The Plant-Based Diet Meal Plan

The Newest 3-Week Kick-Start Guide to Reset & Energize Your Body and Mind; Easy, Healthy, and Whole Foods Delicious Recipes to Eat & Live Your Best.

Italian Recipes Bonus!

Claire Mouyal

Table of Contents

Introduction

Congratulations on purchasing *The Plant-Based Diet Meal Plan,* and thank you for doing so.

While starting a diet can be challenging enough, it is even harder trying to stick with it when life is coming at you from all different Directions. Whether you are dealing with a partner, child, or job responsibility, it is all too easy to put our diets in the back seat!

If you are sick and tired of feeling like junk because you are eating junk, now is the time to make a change! While it may seem like work at first, you have come to the right place to help you get started! Within the chapters of this book, you will be handed everything you need to help you with your new health journey.

In the first few chapters, you will find some delicious, plant-based recipes. Whether you need something for a meal for breakfast, a quick soup to whip together, or a sweet treat at the end of the day, you will find a wide variety of every recipe that you can imagine. I wanted to provide several different types because a plant-based diet should be anything but boring!

When you first begin a plant-based diet, there will be many who question your choices. What many people don't understand is that eating a plant-based diet is natural and our bodies are meant to run on clean energy that plant-based foods provide. Before you know it, you will be losing weight and feeling healthier than ever before.

Obviously, other diets have not been working. Otherwise, you wouldn't be here! Once you have gone through the incredible recipes provided in this book, we will move onto the comprehensive, three-week plan. Here, we will go day-by-day together to help set you up for success! After all, there is no point in following a diet if you are going to go into it blindly.

It is going to take some practice, but it all comes down to creating healthier habits. As you learn the foods, you will be able to enjoy a plant-based diet; it will be easier for you to follow. If you believe in yourself and put in the hard work, you can accomplish anything!

There are plenty of books on this subject on the market, thanks again for choosing this one! Every effort was made to ensure it is full of as much useful information as possible; please enjoy it!

CHAPTER 1:

Breakfast

Chia Seed Breakfast Bowl

Yield: [One]

Prepping: [Fifteen Minutes]

Ingredients

- Chia Seeds [1 t.]
- Peanut Butter [2 t.]
- Blueberries [3 T.]
- Banana [.50, Sliced]
- Almond Milk [.50 C.]
- Coffee [.50 C]
- Old-fashioned Rolled Oats [1 C.]

Directions

1. To start off, you are going to want to take the rolled oats and add them into a bowl with the almond milk and coffee. If you have the time, place in the fridge overnight and permit to soak for several hours.

2. When you are set to serve the meal, layer the chia seeds, blue-berries, sliced banana, and melted peanut butter over the top and enjoy.

Acai Berry Smoothie Bowl

Yield: [Two]

Prepping: [Five Minutes]

Ingredients

- Unsweetened Almond Milk [.25 C.]

- Frozen Mixed Berries [1 C.]

- Frozen Acai [1 C.]

- Old-Fashioned Rolled Oats [.25 C.]

- Banana [1, Sliced]

- Almond Butter [1 T.]

Directions

1. Smoothie bowls are fun to make and fancy to look at! To begin, place all of the items into a food processor and combine until smooth.

2. When you are all set, place the mixture into a serving bowl and top with anything, you would like! Serve immediately.

Plant-Based Breakfast Muffins

Yield: [Six]

Prepping: [Thirty Minutes]

Ingredients

- Unsweetened Almond Milk [2 T.]
- Old-fashioned Oats [2 C.]
- Blueberries [.50 C.]
- Bananas [3, Sliced]
- Chopped Walnuts [.25 C.]

Directions

1. If you are always on the run, these muffins are perfect when you are short on time! Begin by prepping the oven to 350.

2. As the cooker heats, get out a food processor and combine the bananas, almond milk, and oats.

3. When the second step is complete, get out a muffin pan and line it with paper liners.

4. Next, you are going to fill each well and then place the container into the oven for twenty minutes. After this time has passed, remove, and your muffins are ready!

Pumpkin Porridge

Yield: [Two]

Prepping: [One Hour]

Ingredients

- Maple Syrup [4 T.]
- Ground Ginger [.50 t.]
- Pumpkin Puree [.50 C.]
- Ground Clove [.10 t.]
- Ground Cinnamon [1 t.]
- Quinoa [1 C.]

Directions

1. Pumpkin is a flavor that can be enjoyed during any season! To start off, you are going to want to take some time to cook the quinoa according to the Directions on the package. When this is completed, set it to the side.

2. Next, you will want to get out a cooking pan and place it over a high temperature. As this heats, go ahead and put the quinoa along with the rest of the Ingredients. At this point, feel free to alter any seasonings to your own taste.

3. Finally, serve the dish up warm and enjoy your porridge!

Spinach Hash Brown Cakes

Yield: [Four]

Prepping: [Thirty Minutes]

Ingredients

Corn Flour [2 T.]

Onion [.50, Chopped]

Spinach [.50 C., Chopped]

Carrot [1, Grated]

Potatoes [3, Grated]

Salt [Dash]

Chili Powder [.50 t.]

Directions

1. While this breakfast does take some more time, it is easy enough to prep a bunch of these at the beginning of the week, so all you will have to do is heat and go! To start this recipe, you will want to prepare your vegetables as directed and place them in a bowl.

2. Once you have completed step one, you'll want to take a paper towel and remove any excess moisture from the vegetables. When you have done this, go ahead and season to your liking and form patties with your hands.

3. Next, you will take a frying pan and place it over a moderate temperature. After it has heated up, go ahead and splash some water in and begin grilling the patties on both surfaces.

4. When the patties are crispy and cooked through, remove from the stovetop, and enjoy your breakfast.

Sweet Banana Breakfast Cookies

Yield: [Six]

Prepping: [One Hour]

Ingredients

- Unsweetened Applesauce [1 C.]
- Bananas [2]
- Old-Fashioned Oats [1.50 C.]
- Dried Cranberries [.33 C.]
- Cinnamon [Dash]
- Vanilla Extract [1 t.]
- Chopped Walnuts [.25 C.]

Directions

1. It seems strange to have cookies for breakfast, but this is one perk of being an adult! These cookies are on the healthier side and are quick to grab. To get started, prep the stove to 350.

2. Next, you will want to get out your mixing bowl and combine your applesauce with the rest of the Ingredients.

3. Now that you have formed your dough take small amounts and spoon onto a lined cooking sheet. When this step is complete, you are going to pop the dish into the oven for about thirty minutes.

4. After thirty minutes, take the dish out of the oven and let the cookies to chill for five minutes before handing out.

Pancakes Carrot

Yield: [One]

Prepping: [Thirty Minutes]

Ingredients

- Carrots [.25 C., Shredded]
- Ground Cloves [Dash]
- Water [.50 C.]
- Dry Pancake Mix [.50 C.]
- Cinnamon [.25 t.]
- Nutmeg [Dash]

Directions

1. Who doesn't love pancakes in the morning? This recipe helps you get the best of both worlds between a classic breakfast and a boost of nutrition! You'll want to prep by heating a griddle over a moderate temperature.

2. As the griddle warms up, go ahead and take out a small bowl and combine all of the items together until you have formed a mixture. Please note that you may need to add more or less water depending on how many carrots you have.

3. With your mixture created, you will now want to pour the batter onto the heated griddle and grill for about five minutes on either side.

4. When the pancakes are cooked through, remove from the stovetop and serve immediately.

Plant-Based Breakfast Quesadilla

Yield: [Four]

Prepping: [Forty Minutes]

Ingredients

- Extra-firm Tofu [1 Block]
- Green Bell Pepper [1, Diced]
- Red Bell Pepper [1, Diced]
- Onion [.50, Diced]
- Plant-based Cheese [2 C.]
- Whole Wheat Tortillas [4]
- Salt [Dash]
- Pepper [Dash]
- Garlic Powder [.50 t.]
- Turmeric [.50 t.]
- Cumin Powder [.50 t.]

Directions

1. On a morning that you have more time on your hands, it is fun to make these plant-based quesadillas! To begin, you will want to get out a cooking skillet and place it over a moderate temperature. As it warms, add in your vegetables and sauté them together for five minutes. When they are cooked through, take them off of the pan.

2. Now, it is time to cook the tofu. Before you do this, be sure that you have pressed and drained any excess water out of it. When you are set to cook, crumble the tofu with your hands and add the seasoning from the list above to your own taste. Feel free to add more or less seasoning as you feel necessary! Once this is cooked, take this away from the pan as well.

3. When you are set, place one of the tortilla wraps into the bottom of the pan and heat each side for thirty seconds. After both sides are toasty, it is time to assemble the quesadilla! You will put a layer of cheese, followed by the eggs and the vegetables.

4. Now that all of the Ingredients are set, you will want to fold the tortilla over on itself and form the quesadilla. Go ahead and grill each side for an additional couple of minutes, and then it will be all set!

Fluffy Vegetable Chickpea Pancakes

Yield: [Five]

Prepping: [Thirty Minutes]

Ingredients

- Chickpea Flour [2 C.]
- Ground Flax Seed [.25 C.]
- Red Bell Pepper [.50, Chopped]
- Onion [.25, Chopped]
- Spinach [3 C.]
- Roma Tomato [1 C., Chopped]
- Nutritional Yeast [3 T.]
- Salt [Dash]
- Baking Powder [2 t.]
- Unsweetened Almond Milk [1.50 C.]
- Black pepper [Dash]
- Cayenne Pepper [.25 t.]
- Onion Powder [.50 t.]
- Garlic Powder [.50 t.]
- Ground Turmeric [.25 t.]

Directions

1. This recipe is terrific because it packs a protein punch! To begin, you will want to take a cooking skillet out and place it over a moderate heat. Once warm, throw in some water and start cooking your vegetables for five or six minutes. Last-minute, you will want to add the spinach and only cook for a minute. When this step is complete, place your cooked vegetables to the side.

2. Next, you will want to get out your large mixing bowl and combine the seasonings with the nutritional yeast, chickpea flour, baking powder, and the flax meal. When these are combined well, add in the almond milk and stir until mended together well. Once it is, add in the cooked vegetables and stir again.

3. Now that you have your batter, bring the pan back over a moderate heat and scoop a fourth of a cup of your batter into the pan and grill for five minutes for both sides.

4. When you have created all of the batter into pancakes, serve up immediately.

Sweet Strawberry Breakfast Quinoa

Yield: [Four]

Prepping: [Thirty Minutes]

Ingredients

- Unsweetened Almond Milk [2 C.]
- Strawberries [1 C., Sliced]
- Quinoa [1 C.]
- Almonds [2 T., Sliced]
- Unsweetened Coconut Shreds [2 T.]
- Maple Syrup [2 T.]
- Cinnamon [Dash]

Directions

1. For a sweet start for the day, this dish offers a hearty helping of nutrients to get your day off on the right foot. To start off, you will want to go ahead and cook your quinoa in the almond milk according to the Directions on the package. Generally, this should take you about ten to fifteen minutes.

2. Once the quinoa is cooked through, gently add in two more tablespoons of milk along with the dash of cinnamon and maple syrup.

3. With the quinoa made, portion it out into your serving bowls and top with the coconut shreds, sliced almonds, and your strawberry pieces. Enjoy this dish warm or chilled.

Plant-Based French Toast

Yield: [Two]

Prepping: [Thirty Minutes]

Ingredients

- Wheat Bread [5 Slices]
- Unsweetened Almond Milk [1 C.]
- Vanilla Extract [.50 t.]
- Ground Cinnamon [.50 t.]
- Chia Seeds [1 T.]
- Maple Syrup [.50 T.]

Directions

1. Yes, you will still be able to enjoy French toast on a plant-based diet! To begin this simple recipe, you will want to place all of the Ingredients, minus the bread, into a bowl, and place it in the fridge for ten minutes.

2. Next, you will heat a griddle over a moderate heat and begin dipping your bread slices into the batter. Once completely covered, cook on either side for four or five minutes.

3. Once the bread is toasted to your liking, serve with your favorite plant-based toppings and enjoy your breakfast.

Superfood Breakfast Bowl

Yield: [One]

Prepping: [Ten Minutes]

Ingredients

- Unsweetened Almond Milk [1 C.]
- Chia Seeds [.25 C.]
- Old-fashioned Oats [1 C.]
- Cacao Nibs [1 T.]
- Blueberries [.25 C.]
- Vanilla Extract [.50 t.]
- Mulberries [1 T.]
- Goji Berries [1 T.]
- Coconut Flakes [1 T.]

Directions

1. As you can already tell, this recipe is packed to the brim with nutrients! To start out, you will want to cook your oats in the unsweetened almond milk. Once this step is complete, the oatmeal will serve as the base.

2. Next, carefully stir in the chia seeds and the vanilla extract. When the oats are seasoned to your liking, go ahead and layer the rest of the Ingredients over the top. If you want, feel free to add or subtract any of the items in the list above. It is your breakfast, customize however you see fit and then enjoy!

CHAPTER 2:

Salads

Simple Strawberry Salad

Yield: [Three]

Prepping: [Fifteen Minutes]

Ingredients

- Celery [1, Chopped]
- Fennel [1, Chopped]
- Mixed Greens [3 C.]
- Strawberries [2 C., Chopped]

Directions

1. For a fresh and delicious salad, you can't go wrong with this recipe! Before you build your salad, always make sure you rinse and wash your vegetables.

2. When you are set, toss everything in a bowl and serve with your favorite plant-based dressing.

Crunchy Sunflower Salad

Yield: [Four]

Prepping: [Five Minutes]

Ingredients

- Mixed Greens [4 C.]
- Orange [1, Chopped]
- Sunflower Seeds [.25 C.]
- Edamame [1 C.]
- Cranberries [.50 C.]

Directions

1. Looking for a salad with a bit of a crunch? The sunflower seeds will be the perfect addition to any salad!

2. When you are set to assemble your salad, toss all of the items into a salad bowl and enjoy with some dressing drizzled over the top or on the side!

Bell Pepper Salad

Yield: [Eight]

Prepping: [Ten Minutes]

Ingredients

- Mixed Greens [3 C.]
- Red Bell Pepper [2, Diced]
- Onion [.50, Diced]
- Green Bell Pepper [2, Diced]
- Celery [3, Chopped]
- Tomatoes [1, Chopped]

Directions

1. This salad is color, crunchy, and delicious! If you enjoy bell peppers, this is the perfect recipe for you to test out!

2. When you want a fresh, crunchy salad, you will first want to chop up the vegetables according to the Directions listed above. When this is set, go ahead and throw everything into a bowl with your favorite dressing and enjoy it.

Cold Broccoli Slaw Salad

Yield: [Four]

Prepping: [Ten Minutes]

Ingredients

- Broccoli Slaw [3 C.]
- Apples [1 C., Chopped]
- Walnuts [.25 C.]
- Dried Raisins [.25 C.]

Directions

1. While this salad is on the simpler side, it does not lack in flavor! This recipe is perfect for enjoying by itself or as a side salad!

2. When you want to make this salad, I suggest buying broccoli slaw that has already been premade before assembling the salad. Once you have your slaw, you are going to combine all of the items, toss in a salad dressing of your choice, and then you can serve the dish.

Fresh Watercress Salad

Yield: [One]

Prepping: [Ten Minutes]

Ingredients

- Watercress [3 C.]
- Lemon Juice [.50 T.]
- Avocado [1, Sliced]
- Radishes [2, Sliced]
- Cucumber [1, Sliced]

Directions

1. This salad recipe is perfect for those hot, summer days. It has simple Ingredients and will only take a few minutes to put together.

2. Before you toss the salad, be sure to slice up the items according to the Directions in the list above. When this step is complete, throw together your salad with a bit of lemon juice and enjoy it.

Antioxidant Kale Salad

Yield: [Four]

Prepping: [Ten Minutes]

Ingredients

- Kale [3 C.]
- Dried Cranberries [.50 C.]
- Fresh Raspberries [2 C.]
- Blueberries [2 C.]
- Carrots [1, Shredded]
- Almonds [.25 C.]

Directions

1. This salad is lovely to add to any diet because it is full of flavor and offers a boost of nutrition. Before you assemble your salad, make sure you wash the fruit and vegetables.

2. When you are all set, toss together the Ingredients in a mixing bowl, top with your dressing, and your salad is ready to be served.

Citrus Tomato Salad

Yield: [Four]

Prepping: [Ten Minutes]

Ingredients

- Mixed Greens [3 C.]
- Avocado [1, Diced]
- Tomatoes [2 C., Diced]
- Lime Juice [1 T.]
- Onion [.50 C., Diced]
- Parsley [1 T.]

Directions

1. Tomato and lime juice go together surprisingly well! If you are looking for a slightly different salad, give this one a chance!

2. Begin by chopping up the avocado, tomatoes, and onion the way directed and place on top of your mixed greens. Once you have tossed everything together well, you will want to sprinkle the parsley over the top, drip some lime juice in, and then enjoy your salad.

Classic Kale Salad

Yield: [Three]

Prepping: [Ten Minutes]

Ingredients

- Kale [3 C.]
- Pine Nuts [.10 C.]
- Walnuts [.10 C.]
- Quinoa [1 C.]
- Olives [1 C.]

Directions

1. The first step in recreating this salad will be cooking the quinoa. You will want to complete this by following the guidelines that are provided on the package. Generally, this should only take you ten to fifteen minutes. When the quinoa is cooked to your liking, place it into a salad bowl with the rest of the Ingredients.

2. As a final touch, you will want to find a plant-based Caesar dressing or any of your favorites. After you have given the salad a good toss, it will be all set to be served for your next meal.

Creamy Tahini Chickpea Salad

Yield: [Four]

Prepping: [Ten Minutes]

Ingredients

- Tahini Paste [2 T.]
- Chickpeas [1 Can]
- Lemon Juice [2 T.]
- Shallot [1, Minced]
- Pepper [Dash]

Directions

1. This recipe offers an alternative to potato salad or tuna salad. If you like something creamy for your sandwiches or as a side, this recipe is perfect for you.

2. To recreate this salad, you will place your chickpeas into a bowl and gently combine the lemon juice and tahini paste in until the chickpeas are well coated.

3. Once the chickpeas are coated, add in the shallot pieces and dash with pepper to your liking. When the dish is seasoned to your liking, it can be served.

Chilled Winter Salad

Yield: [Five]

Prepping: [Ten Minutes]

Ingredients

- Arugula [3 C.]
- Parsley [2 C.]
- Spinach [3 C.]
- Garlic Cloves [1, Minced]
- Onion [.50, Sliced]
- Cabbage [.50, Shredded]
- Red Wine Vinegar [.33 C.]

Directions

1. Don't let the title fool you; this salad can be enjoyed during any season of the year! It is called a winter salad simply because of the available Ingredients.

2. When you want to make this salad, you can place all of the Ingredients into your serving bowl and toss together. Once this step is complete, add in some red wine vinegar, and it will be ready for your enjoyment.

Simple Superfood Salad

Yield: [Two]

Prepping: [Five Minutes]

Ingredients

- Kale [3 C.]
- Tomatoes [.50 C.]
- Carrots [1, Sliced]
- Blueberries [.25 C.]
- Vinaigrette Salad Dressing [3 T.]

Directions

1. If you need to whip a salad together as quickly as possible, this is going to be the perfect recipe for you to do so.

2. Before you assemble the salad, be sure to slice and dice your tomatoes and carrots beforehand. Once this step is complete, add everything into a bowl and coat with the salad dressing before serving up.

Krunchy Kale Salad

Yield: [Four]

Prepping: [Ten Minutes]

Ingredients

- Kale [3 C.]
- Lemon Juice [3 T.]
- Walnuts [.25 C., Chopped]
- Pear [1, Chopped]
- Pepper [Dash]

Directions

1. It isn't every day that you see fresh pear in a salad! Between the crunch of the walnuts and the citrus flavor of the lemon juice, this salad is very refreshing.

2. All you are going to have to do add all of the items into your bowl, season to your liking, and then it will be set for your enjoyment.

Basic Balsamic Salad Dressing

Yield: [One]

Prepping: [Five Minutes]

Ingredients

- Garlic Cloves [4, Minced]

- Minced Onion [4 T.]

- Dried Basil [3 T.]

- Dried Parsley [3 T.]

- Salt [Dash]

- Balsamic Vinegar [1 C.]

- Water [.25 C.]

Directions

1. As you begin a plant-based diet, you will want to begin cutting out processed foods. You will find out that premade dressings have a lot of additives. Your best bet will be making your own dressing!

2. To make this dressing, you will place everything into your food processor and combine until mixed together well.

Green Avocado Salad Dressing

Yield: [Four]

Prepping: [Five Minutes]

Ingredients

- Lime Juice [1 T.]
- Coconut Milk [1 T.]
- Avocado [1, Sliced]
- Cayenne Pepper [Dash]
- Salt [Dash]
- Pepper [Dash]

Directions

1. If you like your salad dressing on the creamier side, you will absolutely want to give this recipe a taste!

2. Place all of the items in the list above into your food processor and process for thirty seconds or until smooth. After that, adjust your seasonings and use them as you would like!

Citrus Tahini Salad Dressing

Yield: [Five]

Prepping: [Five Minutes]

Ingredients

- Water [.50 C.]
- Lemon Juice [.50 C.]
- Tahini [1 C.]
- Salt [Dash]

Directions

1. As you can tell, this salad dressing is only four Ingredients, but it offers a refreshing flavor fit for any salad.

2. To recreate this tahini salad dressing, pop the items into a food processor and process for several seconds. By the end, everything should be combined well and smooth.

Spiced Ginger Salad Dressing

Yield: [Four]

Prepping: [Five Minutes]

Ingredients

- Apple Cider Vinegar [2 T.]
- Water [.50 C.]
- Maple Syrup [1 T.]
- Pepper [Dash]
- Salt [Dash]
- Fresh Ginger [2 t., Grated]
- Dijon Mustard [2 T.]

Directions

1. While ginger isn't everyone's favorite, it offers a refreshing twist to just about any meal! If you are looking for something new to try, you will want to give this recipe a taste.

2. Simply take all of the items from the list above and put it into your food processor. Once in place, combine until smooth, and your salad dressing will be complete in an instant.

Plant-Based Ranch Salad Dressing

Yield: [Eight]

Prepping: [Ten Minutes]

Ingredients

- Cashews [1 C.]
- Lemon Juice [3 T.]
- Chives [1 T.]
- Dried Parsley [1 T.]
- Onion Powder [.50 t.]
- Garlic Powder [.50 t.]
- Dill [.50 t.]
- Salt [Dash]

Directions

1. Before you start this recipe, you will want to go ahead and soak the cashews in a cup of water for around an hour. By doing this, it will help soften the cashews for blending.

2. When the first step is complete, you are going to want to go ahead and place all of the items into your food processor. Once this is done, blend on high for several seconds and make sure everything is mixed well.

3. Once the dressing is at a consistency you like, season to your taste and enjoy!

CHAPTER 3:

Soups & Stews

Cold Creamy Cucumber Soup

Yield: [Four]

Prepping: [Ten Minutes]

Ingredients

- Avocado [1, Sliced]
- Cucumber [1, Sliced]
- Pepper [Dash]
- Salt [Dash]
- Vegetable Broth [.50 C.]
- Scallion [1, Chopped]
- Lime Juice [1 T.]

Directions

1. When people think of soup, they often think of the meal being hot. This cucumber and avocado soup is creamy, cold, and incredibly refreshing!

2. To recreate this recipe, you will want to go ahead and get out your food processor or blender and place the vegetable broth along with the avocado, cucumber, and the lime juice.

3. When these items are in place, blend until smooth and then place back into the bowl. Once here, sprinkle with pepper and salt to your liking and add in your scallion pieces.

4. You are free to enjoy this immediately, but it tastes even better after chilling in the fridge overnight. Enjoy!

Creamed Cauliflower Soup

Yield: [Four]

Prepping: [Ten Minutes]

Ingredients

- Unsweetened Almond Milk [2 C.]
- Pepper [Dash]
- Garlic Powder [.25 t.]
- Salt [Dash]
- Cauliflower [2 C., Cooked]

Directions

1. Cauliflower acts as an excellent soup base because it gives you a nice, creamy texture. To start this recipe, you are going to want to steam your cauliflower. You can complete this task. However, you typically do. Once the cauliflower is steamed, place it in the fridge and permit it to cool down.

2. Once you can handle the cauliflower, you are going to want to take all of the items from the list above and place it into your food processor or blender. Combine everything together in a high setting for about thirty seconds or until well mixed.

3. Now that you have your soup, you'll want to get your pot out and place it over a moderate temperature. By doing this, you're just heating the soup up before serving.

4. As a final touch, sprinkle some extra seasonings in there and then enjoy your creamy soup.

Spiced Mango Soup

Yield: [Two]

Prepping: [Five Minutes]

Ingredients

- Vegetable Broth [2 C.]
- Ginger Powder [.50 t.]
- Salt [Dash]
- Lime Juice [2 T.]
- Chipotle Powder [1 t.]
- Fresh Mango [2 C.]

Directions

1. Here is another chilled soup to add to your recipe book! Cold soup is an excellent choice as it is easy to prepare and incredibly refreshing on those unforgiving hot days.

2. To create this soup, you will want to take all of the items from the list above and place it into your blender or food processor. Once in place, feel free to adjust the seasonings to your own liking. If you are not a fan of spice, feel free to leave the chipotle out altogether and replace it with something you like better!

3. After you have mended everything together at a high setting, dole out into your serving bowls and enjoy your dish.

Quick and Easy Chickpea Soup

Yield: [Four]

Prepping: [Ten Minutes]

Ingredients

- Vegetable Broth [1 C.]
- Chickpeas [2 Cans]
- Salt [Dash]
- Garlic Cloves [3, Minced]
- Rosemary [1]
- Pepper [Dash]

Directions

1. Chickpeas are incredible in any meal because they offer a higher portion of protein! To begin this recipe, you will first want to take your vegetable broth and chickpeas and put them in your food processor. Go ahead and mix on high until smooth and then set to the side.

2. Next, you will want to take out your soup pot and place it over a moderate temperature. As it warms up, add in a splash of water and the minced garlic cloves. Once you begin to smell the garlic, add in the chickpea liquid and bring everything to a stew.

3. Once the liquid is bubbling, turn the temperature down and allow the soup to simmer for fifteen minutes or until heated thoroughly. When you are all set, season to your liking with the pepper, rosemary, and salt, and your soup will be ready!

Carrot Lentil Soup

Yield: [Four]

Prepping: [Twenty Minutes]

Ingredients

- Vegetable Broth [8 C.]
- Garlic Clove [1, Minced]
- Pepper [Dash]
- Carrots [6, Chopped]
- Red Lentils [2 C.]
- Salt [Dash]

Directions

1. This soup is excellent by itself or served with a simple side salad. To start off, you will want to take out your soup pot and place it over a moderate temperature.

2. As the pot warms up, add in the garlic and sauté for several minutes. Once you begin to smell the garlic, you can add in the rest of the Ingredients and take the soup to a boil.

3. Once the soup is bubbling, turn the heat down and allow the soup to simmer for twenty minutes. After twenty minutes, feel free to remove the carrots and garlic. You can also leave them for more of a stew feel.

4. Finally, sprinkle some extra seasoning over the top and enjoy your soup.

Easy Pumpkin Soup

Yield: [Four]

Prepping: [Twenty Minutes]

Ingredients

- Unsweetened Almond Milk [2 C.]
- Pumpkin Puree [4 C.]
- Maple Syrup [1 T.]
- Salt [Dash]
- Optional: Red Pepper Flakes [Dash]

Directions

1. If you are a fan of pumpkin, you are really going to enjoy the soup! It is quick to make and easy to enjoy. You'll want to start by taking out a soup pot and placing it over a moderate temperature.

2. As the pot warms up, place the pumpkin in your food processor along with the almond milk and maple syrup. Once these items are in place, give them a good mix to mend together smoothly.

3. Now, you are going to add the mix into the pot and bring it to a stew. Once bubbling, lower the temperature and cook for an additional fifteen minutes.

4. Finally, sprinkle a dash of salt, and some red pepper flakes in, and your soup will be set for your enjoyment.

Basic Vegetable Stew

Yield: [Four]

Prepping: [Twenty Minutes]

Ingredients

- Balsamic Vinegar [2 T.]
- Vegetable Broth [1 C.]
- Eggplant [1, Diced]
- Zucchini [2, Diced]
- Salt [Dash]
- Grape Tomatoes [1 C., Halved]
- Pepper [Dash]

Directions

1. As you can see, this recipe only requires a handful of Ingredients. This recipe is perfect for when you want to whip together a healthy meal. You'll start off by taking a sauté pan and placing it over a moderate temperature. As it heats up, sprinkle some water in there and then add in the eggplant and zucchini pieces. You will only need to sauté these items for five minutes or so.

2. Once these vegetables are soft, you will want to add in the tomatoes and any seasonings that you desire. When the tomatoes are cooked to your liking, add in the vegetable broth and allow it to cook down for an additional five minutes.

3. As a final touch, add in the balsamic vinegar and any additional seasonings you feel necessary for the dish. When you are finished, your stew will be set for serving.

Spiced Chickpea Stew

Yield: [Four]

Prepping: [Thirty Minutes]

Ingredients

- Chickpeas [2 C.]
- Tomatoes [1 C., Diced]
- Garlic Clove [1, Minced]
- Onion [1, Diced]
- Lemon Juice [1 T.]
- Coriander Leaves [1 T.]
- Garam Masala [2 t.]
- Green Chilies [2, Chopped]

Directions

1. If you are looking for a meal that has a spicy kick to it, this is going to be the recipe for you! To begin, you will want to get out a cooking pan and place it over a moderate heat. As it warms, throw in some water and begin sautéing the onion and garlic together.

2. As you begin to smell the garlic and the onion gets soft, you will want to add in the green chilies, tomatoes, and chickpeas. Go ahead and sauté these items for an additional five minutes.

3. Now that the vegetables are cooked through go ahead and gently stir in the garam masala and the lemon juice. At this point, feel free to season the stew to your liking.

4. When you are all set to serve, portion the stew out and garnish with some fresh cilantro for an extra boost of flavor.

Turmeric Lentil Stew

Yield: [Two]

Prepping: [Thirty Minutes]

Ingredients

- Vegetable Broth [6 C.]
- Carrots [2, Chopped]
- Garlic Cloves [2, Minced]
- Onion [.50, Chopped]
- Pepper [Dash]
- Cumin [2 t.]
- Turmeric [2 t.]
- Salt [Dash]
- Brown Lentils [1 C.]

Directions

1. While lentils do take a little bit longer to cook, they are another great source of protein for your diet. Whether you are looking to enjoy this meal for lunch or dinner, it is relatively simple to create!

2. You will start this recipe off by heating a soup pot over a moderate temperature. When it is warm enough, add in the garlic cloves and onion. You will sauté these items for three or four minutes.

3. Once the second step is complete, add in the vegetable broth along with the lentils and the carrot pieces. When these are in place, bring the items to a stew and then turn the heat down and simmer everything for twenty minutes.

4. After this time has passed, the lentils should be cooked through and fluffy. If they are prepared to your liking, gently stir in your seasonings, and then your soup will be set for serving.

Curried Coconut Stew

Yield: [Four]

Prepping: [Thirty Minutes]

Ingredients

- Coconut Milk [1, 14 Oz. Can]
- Zucchini [1, Sliced]
- Onion [1, Diced]
- Chickpeas [2 Cans]
- Curry Powder [2 T.]
- Salt [Dash]

Directions

1. This meatless, vegetable stew is versatile and healthy. To start, you will want to get out your cooking skillet and place it over a moderate temperature. As it warms up, sprinkle in some water and add the onion. You will want to go ahead and cook the onion for five minutes or until it is soft.

2. When the onion is cooked, add in the zucchini and sauté for an additional five minutes. When the zucchini is soft as well, you will want to sprinkle in the curry powder and pour in the coconut milk. Once the items are bubbling, turn the heat down and allow the Ingredients to simmer for fifteen minutes.

3. After fifteen minutes, drain your chickpeas and then add them into the heated skillet. You will want to heat these for approximately five or six more minutes.

4. Finally, portion out your stew and season to your liking before enjoying your hot meal.

Irish Vegetable Stew

Yield: [Six]

Prepping: [Thirty Minutes]

Ingredients

- Vegetable Broth [4 C.]
- Garlic Cloves [3, Minced]
- Carrots [2, Chopped]
- Celery [2, Chopped]
- Onion [1, Chopped]
- Potatoes [1 C., Chopped]
- Mushrooms [1 C., Chopped]
- Plant-based Flour [.25 C.]
- Stout Beer [1 C.]
- Tomato Paste [.25 C.]
- Pepper [Dash]
- Brown Sugar [2 t.]
- Bay Leaf [1]
- Salt [Dash]
- Thyme [1 t.]

Directions

1. Traditionally, Irish stew is made with Guinness and Lamb. On the plant-based diet, we have to change some of the Ingredients, but you can still enjoy a hearty Irish stew. As you can tell, this stew has quite a few Ingredients, but after you have gotten through all of the chopping, the stew is reasonably easy to cook! With that said, get to chopping!

2. When your vegetables are chopped and ready, you will want to get out the largest pot you own and place it over a moderate-high temperature. As it warms, throw some water into the bottom and begin sautéing the garlic, onion, and celery pieces for five minutes.

3. After these veggies have cooked through, you are going to toss in the flour and coat the cooked vegetables. Be sure that everything is covered before adding in two cups of your vegetable broth.

4. When the first three steps are completed, pour in the beer, spices, tomato paste, and the rest of your vegetables. Please note that the beer is going to foam up; this is the alcohol cooking out! Now, bring the stew to a gentle simmer and cook it for an additional fifteen minutes.

5. If you like a thinner stew, you will want to consider adding in an extra cup of broth, or two. When it is to your liking, remove the bay leaf from the stew, and it will be set for your enjoyment!

Lentil and Butternut Squash Stew

Yield: [Four]

Prepping: [One Hour]

Ingredients

- Vegetable Broth [2 C.]
- Lentils [.50 C.]
- Carrots [2, Diced]
- Spinach [2 C.]
- Butternut Squash [1, Diced]
- Garlic Cloves [2, Minced]
- Fresh Ginger [1 t.]
- Apple [1, Diced]
- Cayenne Pepper [Dash]
- Salt [Dash]
- Tomato Paste [1 T.]
- Curry Powder [1 T.]
- Pepper [Dash]
- Onion [1, Diced]

Directions

1. It's not every day you find apples in your stew! The flavors of this recipe genuinely complement one another. While it does take a bit longer to make, this is the perfect recipe to batch for the week! You can begin by taking out your stew pot and placing it over a moderate-high temperature.

2. As the pot warms, add in the carrots and onion. Go ahead and sauté these items for five minutes before adding in the curry powder, tomato paste, garlic, and ginger. At this point, you will sauté the Ingredients for an additional minute.

3. Once the first two steps are completed, you will then place the vegetable broth and lentils into the pot and get everything to a soft simmer. At this point, you'll want to put the lid on and permit the Ingredients to stew for twenty-five minutes.

4. After this time had passed, you will now toss the squash and apple pieces into the pot and cook for twenty minutes more. Please note that you may need to add additional broth when you add in the extra Ingredients.

5. Finally, you will want to season the stew to your liking and add in the spinach last minute before portioning your meal out. Once the spinach has wilted, that is when you know your meal is ready!

CHAPTER 4:

Lunch

Classic French Dip Sandwich

Yield: [Two]

Prepping: [Forty-five Minutes]

Ingredients

- Vegetable Broth [1 C.]
- Garlic Clove [1, Minced]
- Onion [1, Sliced]
- Portobello Mushroom Caps [3, Sliced]
- Sandwich Rolls [2]
- Pepper [Dash]
- Soy Sauce [1 T.]
- Liquid Smoke [.25 t.]
- Plant-based Worcestershire Sauce [1 T.]
- Thyme [.25 t.]
- Salt [Dash]

Directions

1. The French dip sandwich is a classic lunch favorite, and now you can enjoy a plant-based version of it! To start off, you will want to take out your cooking skillet and place it over a moderate temperature. As it heats, add in a sprinkle of water and the onion. Go ahead and cook the onion for twenty minutes. As you do this, be sure to keep stirring to avoid anything burning to the bottom. Last-minute, you are going to sauté the garlic with the onion for thirty seconds and then remove both items.

2. Next, it is time to sauté the mushrooms. Toss some more water into the pan to help keep the mushrooms from burning and cook these for ten minutes. You will want to keep flipping the mushrooms to cook them more thoroughly. After the mushrooms are heated to your liking, add the onions back into the pan.

3. Now that these items are in place, it is time to add the pepper, liquid smoke, vegetable broth, Worcestershire sauce, thyme, and soy sauce. When these items are put in the pan, cook for an additional five minutes.

4. When you are set to assemble your sandwich, you'll want to take some time to squeeze the excess juices out of the onion and mushroom mixture before layering into your rolls; this will be the dip part of the French dip!. For a final touch, top with some mustard and enjoy your lunch!

Simple Hummus and Vegetable Sandwich

Yield: [One]

Prepping: [Five Minutes]

Ingredients

- Hummus [4 T.]
- Cucumber [.25 C., Sliced]
- Carrots [.50 C., Shredded]
- Avocado [.50, Smashed]
- Whole Wheat Bread [2 Slices]
- Mixed Greens [.50 C.]
- Green Bell Pepper [.50, Sliced]

Directions

1. If you are in a hurry but still want a nutritious, plant-based lunch, this is an excellent recipe for you to test out. Before you assemble your sandwich, you will want to take the time to chop and slice the vegetables according to the Directions above.

2. When the vegetables are cut up, take the slices of bread and spread your hummus on either side. Once this step is complete, build your sandwich; however, you would like, and then it will be ready for your meal!

Green Pesto Melted Sandwich

Yield: [One]

Prepping: [Ten Minutes]

Ingredients

- Whole Wheat Bread [2 Sliced]
- Arugula [.50 C.]
- Plant-based Pesto [2 T.]
- Avocado [.50, Sliced]
- Cannellini Beans [.50 C.]
- Artichoke Hearts [2, Chopped]
- Pepper [Dash]

Directions

1. As you can tell from the name, this sandwich is packed to the brim with green nutrients! Luckily, it is easy to make so that you can get to the good part; eating! You are going to want to start off by taking out a good-sized mixing bowl and begin mashing the beans down. Once they are chunky, stir in the pesto and spread that mixture onto your bread.

2. Now, it is time to build the sandwich. You can do this any way you like, but the cleanest way will be artichoke hearts down first, followed by the arugula and avocado slices. At this point, feel free to add some more pesto in between and season to your liking.

3. Next, you'll want to take out your griddle and place it over a moderate temperature. Once it is warm, add the sandwich and grill each side for five minutes or until crispy.

4. Finally, cut the sandwich in half, and enjoy with a nice side salad!

Smokey Tofu Sandwich

Yield: [Two]

Prepping: [Ten Minutes]

Ingredients

- Whole Wheat Bread [4 Slices]
- Alfalfa Sprouts [1 C.]
- Avocado [1, Sliced]
- Dijon Mustard [2 T.]
- Smoked Tofu [1 Package]
- Red Bell Pepper [1. Roasted]

Directions

1. The good news is that as the plant-based diet grows in popularity, more products are coming to the store! With that being said, you will want to go ahead and pick up smoked tofu during your next trip to the store for this recipe.

2. When you are ready to assemble your sandwich, you will first want to take your tofu and slice it down the long side to make thinner pieces. Once this step is complete, get out a cooking skillet and bring it over a moderate temperature. Once warm, begin browning the tofu on both sides for about five or six minutes.

3. Next, you will want to lay out the bread slices and carefully place the tofu on top of one of the slices. When the tofu is placed, begin layering the rest of your Ingredients and top off with a bit of Dijon mustard.

4. Finally, slice your sandwich in half and serve it up warm!

Simple Chickpea Salad Sandwich

Yield: [Four]

Prepping: [Twenty Minutes]

Ingredients

- Chickpeas [1 Can]
- Vegan Mayo [.25 C.]
- Salt [Dash]
- Lettuce [4 Leaves]
- Whole Wheat Bread [8 Slices]
- Dill [.25 t.]
- Onion [.25 C., Chopped]
- Bell Pepper [.50 C., Chopped]
- Celery [1, Chopped]
- Sweet Pickle Relish [2 T.]

Directions

1. If you liked tuna salad when you were following a SAD diet, you will absolutely adore this recipe! You will want to begin by draining the can of chickpeas and placing them into a mixing bowl. Once in place, go ahead and mash them down with a masher before adding in the rest of the Ingredients.

2. When you are set to assemble your sandwich, you will next lay out the bread slices and carefully spread a light layer of mayo on both sides. Once this is complete, top one side with the lettuce leaf and spread the chickpea over the surface. Finally, close the sandwich, chop it in half, and enjoy your creamy, chickpea salad sandwich!

Falafel and Hummus Hero

Yield: [Four]

Prepping: [Thirty Minutes]

Ingredients

- Hummus [1 Container]
- Cilantro [2 T.]
- White Beans [1 Can]
- Plant-based Flour [.50 C.]
- Breadcrumbs [1 C.]
- Whole Wheat Rolls [4]
- Cucumber [1, Sliced]
- Tomatoes [1, Sliced]
- Mixed Greens [.50 C.]

Directions

1. Believe it or not, it is fairly simple to make your own falafel balls! To begin this process, you will first want to take the container of hummus and place all of the contents into your food processor. With this in place, you will next add in the cilantro, plant-based flour, and the beans. Now that all of these items are in place go ahead and pulse the Ingredients until they are mended together.

2. With the first step complete, you will want to roll the dough with your hands into small balls and roll around in the breadcrumbs. Once you have completed this step, you can place the balls to the side.

3. Next, heat up a pan over a moderate temperature. Once warm, add in your falafel balls and grill them for five minutes on each side. By the end, the falafels should be browned and crispy.

4. When the falafels are all set, you will now want to take the time to spread some extra hummus on your roll and toast them in the stove for a couple of minutes; this will help add some texture to your sandwich.

5. Finally, layer the falafel balls with the sliced vegetables, and your hero will be set for lunch!

Raw Veggie Wrap

Yield: [Four]

Prepping: [Fifteen Minutes]

Ingredients

- Large Lettuce Wraps [4]
- Zucchini [1, Sliced]
- Carrot [3, Sliced]
- Avocado [1, Sliced]
- Lemon Juice [2 T.]
- Beet [2, Sliced]

Directions

1. If you are short on time and need a quick lunch, this recipe only has a handful of Ingredients and can be ready in an instant! You will want to begin by slicing up the vegetables. For these wraps, try your best to slice the vegetables into thin strips.

2. Next, it is time to mash up the avocado in a mixing bowl. Once it is smooth, stir in the lemon juice and mend these two Ingredients together well. When it is set, spread the avocado along with the lettuce wraps and begin layering your vegetables.

3. As you wrap up the lettuce, try to do this as tightly as possible without tearing the lettuce. For easier eating, try placing the wraps into the fridge for five minutes before enjoying it.

Loaded Plant-Based Nachos

Yield: [Four]

Prepping: [Thirty Minutes]

Ingredients

- Whole Grain Tortilla Chips [2 C.]
- Red Bell Pepper [.50, Chopped]
- Jalapeno Pepper [.50, Chopped]
- Onion [.50, Chopped]
- Mushrooms [2 C., Chopped]
- Toasted Walnuts [1 C., Halved]
- Plant-based Cheese [.50 C.]
- Garlic Powder [.25 t.]
- Cumin [1 t.]
- Salt [Dash]
- Smoked Paprika [1 t.]
- Chili Powder [1 t.]
- Lime Juice [1 T.]
- Cumin [1 t.]
- Chipotle Peppers [.25 t.]

Directions

1. While you won't be eating traditional nachos anymore, this is an excellent plant-based alternative to try out! Before you begin assembling your nachos, you will want to go ahead and prep the stove to 400 and get out your cooking sheet and line it.

2. Next, it is time to make the "meat" for the nachos. You can complete this task by placing the mushrooms and walnuts into your food processor. As you pulse these items together, the mix should become crumbled.

3. When the mushroom mix is set, go ahead and place it into a skillet over a low temperature. As it heats up, add in the seasonings along with the jalapeno and the onion. Generally, this should take about ten minutes or until the peppers are soft.

4. Now, it is time to assemble the nachos! Go ahead and lay out the tortilla chips onto your cooking sheet and top with the "meat" and any other vegetables you would like on your nachos.

5. With these items set, sprinkle your plant-based cheese over the top and pop into the stove for ten minutes. By the end of this time, the cheese should be melted, and your nachos can be served warm!

Masala Mushrooms

Yield: [Four]

Prepping: [Twenty Minutes]

Ingredients

- Mushrooms [1 C.]
- Curry Leaves [2]
- Ginger Garlic Paste [1 t.]
- Onion [.50 C., Chopped]
- Green Peas [.25 C.]
- Green Chili [1, Chopped]
- Garam Masala [1 t.]
- Turmeric [Dash]
- Red Chili Powder [Dash]
- Lemon Juice [1 t.]
- Mustard [.25 t.]

Directions

1. If you want lunch on the spicier side, this mushroom marsala can be served by itself, on a slice of bread, or over a bed of rice. To begin this recipe, you will want to take a larger cooking pan and place it over a moderate heat. As it warms up, you will first want to begin frying the garlic ginger paste with the mustard and the cumin. You will do this for approximately two to three minutes.

2. Next, you will add in the chopped onions and cook those for five minutes. After this time has passed, add in the mushroom and tomato pieces before tossing in the seasonings. As you prepare these items, be sure not to overcook the mushrooms as they can become very soggy.

3. For a final touch, feel free to add in some lemon juice, and then after five minutes, your mushroom masala will be set for your meal.

Cauliflower Nuggets

Yield: [One]

Prepping: [One Hour]

Ingredients

- Chickpea Flour [.50 C.]
- Cauliflower Florets [2 C.]
- Water [.25 C.]
- Hot Sauce [4 T.]

Directions

1. This recipe is incredible because the cauliflower nuggets are easy to make, low in carbs, and absolutely addicting! You will want to start this simple recipe off by heating the stove to 350. Also, get out your cooking sheet and line it, for easy cleanup.

2. Next, you will want to get out the cauliflower pieces and layer them evenly across the sheet. Once in place, you will pop the dish into the cooker for thirty minutes. By the end, the cauliflower should be crispy on the edges.

3. As the cauliflower cooks, you can go ahead and get out a mixing bowl. Here, you will want to toss together the hot sauce, water, and flour. This mixture will create your batter.

4. After thirty minutes, remove the dish from the oven and carefully dip each cauliflower piece into the batter before replacing it onto the cooking sheet.

5. Once the cauliflower pieces have all been covered, pop the dish back into the stove for an additional thirty minutes, and by the end, you should have crispy nuggets!

Sweet Pea Nuggets

Yield: [Four]

Prepping: [Ten Minutes]

Ingredients

- Plant-based Flour [2 T.]
- Old-fashioned Rolled Oats [4 T.]
- Sweet and Sour Chili Sauce [2 T.]
- Breadcrumbs [4 T.]
- Salt [Dash]
- Frozen Peas [1 C.]
- Sundried Tomatoes [2, Chopped]

Directions

1. While following a plant-based diet, it is going to be important to have a wide variety of recipes to help keep your diet new and exciting! I bet you have never heard of sweet pea nuggets before! Luckily, this recipe is super easy!

2. To begin, you will want to take all of the items from the list above and place it into your food processor. Here, you will create a dough mixture. Once this is complete, use your hands to form nuggets and then set it to the side.

3. When you are ready to cook your nuggets, take a griddle and place it over a moderate temperature. Once warm, put the nuggets in and grill for approximately five minutes on either side. By the end, the nuggets should be crispy and are excellent for dipping!

Spicy 'Chicken' Wraps

Yield: [Four]

Prepping: [Ten Minutes]

Ingredients

- Whole Wheat Wraps [4]
- Tomato [1, Diced]
- Hot Sauce [.25 C.]
- Seitan [1 Package, Chopped]
- Kale [1 C.]
- Unsweetened Almond Milk [8 T.]
- Apple Cider Vinegar [2 T.]
- Salt [Dash]
- Dried Parsley [.50 t.]
- Pepper [Dash]
- Dried Dill [.50 t.]
- Cashews [1 C.]

Directions

1. If you enjoy buffalo chicken wraps, this will be your perfect, plant-based alternative. If you have never tried seitan before, this is a great starter recipe for you. Much like tofu, seitan takes on the flavor of anything it is cooked in though the texture can be strange for people at first.

2. To begin this recipe, you will want to start out by making your plant-based ranch dressing. In order to start this process, you will want to soak your cashews for about thirty minutes beforehand. Once the cashews are soft, you will want to add the cashews, dried dill, dried parsley, almond milk, apple cider vinegar, and a dash of pepper into a food processor and mend until smooth. When this step is finished, set the sauce to the side.

3. When you are set, it is time to grill the seitan. For this, take out a grilling pan and put it over a moderate heat. Once warm, add in the seitan and cook for ten minutes. Halfway through, you will want to flip the seitan over. Once cooked through, go ahead and add in the buffalo sauce and let the seitan soak up the flavor.

4. With these items set, it is time to assemble your wraps. Begin by laying out each wrap and spread a couple of tablespoons of ranch across the surface. When this is set, layer the kale and tomato and finally place the seitan on. Go ahead and wrap it up tight, cut in half, and your wrap will be set for your enjoyment.

CHAPTER 5:

Snacks & Appetizers

Hot and Spicy Chickpea Poppers

Yield: [Four]

Prepping: [One Hour]

Ingredients

- Chickpeas [2 C.]
- Garlic Powder [.50 t.]
- Chili Powder [1 t.]
- Lime Juice [.50 T.]

Directions

1. Whether you are looking for an appetizer, a quick snack, or something to throw on top of your salad, these chickpea poppers are filled with flavor! To start, you will want to prep your cooker to 400 and line a sheet with baking paper.

2. Next, get out a mixing bowl so you can combine the chickpeas with the lime juice and seasoning.

3. Once the chickpeas are covered to your liking, layer them across the sheet and pop into the oven for about an hour. For extra-crispy chickpeas, stir them every twenty minutes or so.

Loaded Plant-Based Quesadillas

Yield: [Four]

Prepping: [Forty Minutes]

Ingredients

- Whole Wheat Tortillas [6]
- Black Beans [1 C.]
- Zucchini [1, Chopped]
- Red Bell Pepper [1, Sliced]
- Jalapeno Pepper [1, Sliced]
- Avocado [1, Sliced]
- Salt [Dash]
- Garlic Clove [1, Minced]
- Pepper [Dash]
- Ground Cumin [1 T.]
- Lime Juice [2 T.]
- Chile Powder [.50 t.]
- Maple Syrup [1 t.]
- Onion [.50, Chopped]

Directions

1. What is better than a quesadilla? A loaded quesadilla! To start this recipe, get out a large bowl so that you can mix together the pepper, salt, chili powder, cumin, and the lime juice. After you have added a couple of teaspoons of water, add in your chopped vegetable and marinate for around an hour.

2. When your vegetables are flavored enough, get out a cooking skillet and place it over a moderate heat. As it warms, add the flavored vegetables and cook for five minutes. Once the veggies are soft, you can add in your beans and cook for an additional five minutes. When this step is complete, place the veggies to the side.

3. Next, you will want to get out your avocado and begin mashing it down in a small bowl. Once it is smooth, spread it over half of your quesadilla and season with some pepper and salt. If you like your quesadillas spicy, feel free to add hot sauce at this point, as well.

4. When you are set, layer the cooked vegetables in the folded half of the quesadilla and close it up. You will want to repeat these steps until you have the number of quesadillas you need.

5. Finally, you are going to take your skillet back over a moderate heat and begin grilling the quesadillas on either side. Generally, this will take about five minutes per side. By the end, the bottoms should be grilled and crispy.

6. Finally, serve with some salsa, and your snack is ready for you.

Stuffed Garlic Mushrooms

Yield: [Ten]

Prepping: [One Hour]

Ingredients

- Mushroom Caps [10]
- Lemon Juice [.50 t.]
- Garlic Clove [1, Mashed]
- Salt [Dash]
- Italian Parsley [1 T.]
- Fresh Herbs [1 t.]

Directions

1. When looking for a quick bite, mushrooms are an excellent choice. Mushrooms are packed with nutritional value, and they are tasty to eat! To begin this recipe, you will first need to prepare the mushroom caps. You can accomplish this by rinsing the mushrooms and carefully remove the stems.

2. Next, you will want to get out a small mixing bowl and mash together the herbs, garlic, and a dash of salt. Once you have made a paste out of these Ingredients, place it in with the parsley and lemon juice.

3. Now that you have made your marinade add in the mushrooms and allow them to sit at room temperature for around twenty minutes. As the mushrooms soak, you will want to go ahead and prep the stove to 400.

4. When you are set to bake your snack, get out a cooking sheet, and line the mushrooms evenly across the surface. When this is complete, pop the dish into the oven for thirty minutes. By the end, the mushrooms should be browned on the edges.

5. Remove from the oven, put some salt over the top, and enjoy.

Pizza Quinoa Snack Balls

Yield: [Four]

Prepping: [Forty Minutes]

Ingredients

- Quinoa [1 C., Cooked]
- Tomato Paste [.33 C.]
- Italian Seasoning [2 T.]
- Basil Leaves [5]
- Red Beans [1 C.]
- Parsley [.25 C., Chopped]

Directions

1. If you enjoy pizza, but you do not have time to make a whole pizza, these pizza snack balls are perfect for any day of the week! Before you begin this recipe, you will want to go ahead and cook the quinoa according to the Directions on the package. Generally, this will only take you fifteen to twenty minutes, depending on the brand.

2. When the quinoa has been cooked, take out a medium-sized mixing bowl and mend all of the items from the list above, together. If you would like, feel free to adjust the seasonings to your own taste. At the end of this step, you will have a dough-like texture.

3. Next, you can use your hands to make balls from the dough and place them into the fridge for five to ten minutes. As you wait, you will want to prep the cooker to 350 and line a cooking sheet.

4. When you are ready to make the balls, you are going to spread them on your cooking sheet and pop them into the oven for about thirty minutes. At the end of this time, your pizza balls will be firm and crispy. Serve with some marinara sauce and enjoy your snack.

Easy Baked Carrot Chips

Yield: [Eight]

Prepping: [Forty Minutes]

Ingredients

- Carrots [3, Sliced Thin]
- Water [.25 C.]
- Ground Cinnamon [1 t.]
- Salt [Dash]
- Chili Powder [1 t.]

Directions

1. Every once in a while, we want something crunchy! With carrot chips, this is an excellent way to satisfy that craving and still stick with your diet. Before you begin prepping your carrots, you can turn the cooker to 425.

2. Next, you will want to trim the carrot tops off and begin slicing them up. To make this step a bit easier, consider using a mandolin slicer on the smallest setting. As you slice up your carrots, place them into a mixing bowl along with the water and seasoning. If you don't like spice, feel free to mix up the seasonings however you would like!

3. When the carrots are seasoned to your liking, you will next layer them on a baking sheet and pop into the oven for fifteen minutes. As you cook the carrots, be sure that you are keeping an eye on them. When the carrots are cooking, you will notice that the edges are going to curl up and crisp; this is perfectly normal.

4. After fifteen minutes, flip the carrots over and cook for an additional ten minutes. Once the whole carrot is crispy, remove from oven and allow to chill thoroughly before enjoying your snack.

Basic Energy Snack Bar

Yield: [Four]

Prepping: [Five Minutes]

Ingredients

- Chia Seeds [1 T.]
- Flax Seeds [1 T.]
- Dates [1 C.]
- Raisins [1 C.]
- Almonds [.50 C.]
- Maple Syrup [2 T.]

Directions

1. As a busy person, you probably have very little time to sit down and make yourself a snack. Luckily, you can make these quick and easy energy snack bars when you need them most!

2. The first step for your energy bars will be placing the almonds and dates into a food processor and pulsing together. Once you have a paste, you can add in the rest of the Ingredients and create the "dough" for your energy bars.

3. When this step is complete, you will want to get out a square dish and line it with your handy-dandy parchment paper. Once in place, add the mixture into the dish and press down with your palms.

4. Once the bars are in their place, pop the dish into the fridge for at least two hours before slicing and serving. As stated earlier, this is the perfect recipe to make at the beginning of the week, so you have a snack whenever you need it.

Cheese Kale Bites

Yield: [Three]

Prepping: [One Hour]

Ingredients

- Kale [3 C.]
- Cashews [1 C.]
- Nutritional Yeast [.33 C.]
- Soy Sauce [1 T.]
- Water [2 T.]
- Lemon Juice [1 T.]
- Garlic Clove [1. Minced]
- Red Bell Pepper [.50, Chopped]

Directions

1. As you already know, a plant-based diet offers a variety of different flavors. You may not be eating traditional cheese on your new diet, but it will taste very close! Before you begin this recipe, you will want to soak your cashews for at least an hour ahead of time so that they will become nice and soft.

2. When you are set to make your chips, you can go ahead and line your cooking sheets and turn your stove to the lowest heat setting possible. As the oven heats, you can drain the cashews and begin breaking the kale pieces up into bite-sized pieces.

3. Next, you will want to get out your food processor and mend together the lemon juice, water, nutritional yeast, garlic, soy sauce, and the soaked cashews. Once you have created a paste, you will mix that into a bowl with your kale and cover evenly.

4. Now that your kale has become "cheesy," you will lay the pieces across the surface of the cooking sheet and place it into the stove for three hours. After an hour, you will want to check on the kale and flip it over.

5. By the end of the three hours, you will have crunchy chips, ready for snack time.

Peanut Butter Snack Bites

Yield: [Twenty]

Prepping: [Forty Minutes]

Ingredients

- Quinoa [.50 C.]

- Molasses [.50 t.]

- Cinnamon [.50 t.]

- Maple Syrup [1 t.]

- Peanut Butter [.50 C.]

- Salt [Dash]

Directions

1. When you need something on the go, it is easier to be able to grab something that is already packaged. These peanut butter snack balls are bite-sized and will be ready whenever you need them! To start this recipe off, you will want to go ahead and cook the quinoa according to the Directions provided on the package. Once it is soft and fluffy, set it to the side and allow it to chill out completely.

2. Now that you are set to make your snack bites, you will want to get out your mixing bowl and mend the quinoa with the rest of the Ingredients. Once you have a dough, use your hands to roll one-inch balls and then place them in the fridge.

3. Once the balls are firm, they will be set for your enjoyment!

Spicy Sweet Potato Fries

Yield: [Two]

Prepping: [Thirty Minutes]

Ingredients

- Sweet Potato [2]
- Water [2 T.]
- Chipotle Pepper [1 t.]
- Garlic powder [.50 t.]
- Salt [Dash]

Directions

1. If you need something as a quick snack or an appetizer before dinner, these sweet potato fries really do hit the spot! To start out, you will want to wash your sweet potatoes well and then slice them up into fries. After the fries have been cut, prep the stove to 425.

2. Next, you will place your freshly cut fries into a mixing bowl and combine with the water and the seasoning. Be sure to toss well to coat the fries completely.

3. When you are set, line the fries up on the surface of your cooking sheet and pop the dish into the stove for fifteen minutes. After fifteen minutes, you will turn the fries and bake them for an additional fifteen minutes.

4. Once the fries are crispy to your liking, remove from the oven and permit to chill for five minutes before enjoying them.

CHAPTER 6:

Dinner

Fried Thai Quinoa

Yield: [Six]

Prepping: [Thirty Minutes]

Ingredients

- Quinoa [2 C.]
- Ginger [2 T., Chopped]
- Green Beans [1 Can]
- Red Bell Pepper [2, Chopped]
- Extra-firm Tofu [1 Package, Cubed]
- Water [3 T.]
- Red Curry Paste [2 T.]
- Soy Sauce [.25 C.]

Directions

1. If you are looking for a one-pot dinner, this is an excellent place to start! You will want to begin this recipe by cooking the quinoa according to the instructions on the package. When this is done, set the quinoa to the side.

2. In the same skillet, add the tofu and chopped vegetables in, along with a tablespoon of water and cook for around ten minutes. Once the vegetables are tender, you can add in the quinoa and reduce the temperature a bit.

3. Now, it is time to make the sauce for your dinner. For this, you will just have to add in the soy sauce, curry paste, and the water. If you want, feel free to add a touch more water to make a thinner sauce.

4. Once you have added the sauce into your skillet, stir everything consistently to help spread the flavors across the other items. After you have cooked for an additional ten minutes, pepper on some sesame seeds, and dinner is served.

Simple Spiced Brown Rice

Yield: [Six]

Prepping: [Fifteen Minutes]

Ingredients

- Black Beans [1 Can]
- Roasted Corn [2 C.]
- Brown Rice [2 C.]
- Avocado [.50, Sliced]
- Chili Powder [1 T.]

Directions

1. While some people may consider this dish aside, it also serves as a basic dinner when you are short on time [or groceries!]

2. To recreate this dish, you will first want to cook the brown rice according to the Directions provided on the package. When this is set, you now have the base of your dish.

3. To complete your meal, layer the black beans and corn on top of the brown rice and sprinkle the chili powder over the top. For some added texture, slice up an avocado, and your meal is ready in an instant.

Tomato and Zoodles

Yield: [Four]

Prepping: [30 Minutes]

Ingredients

- Zucchini Squash or Zoodles [1 or 3 C.]
- Small Tomatoes [1 C., Chopped]
- Onion [1, Sliced]
- White Balsamic Vinegar [1 T.]
- Water [4 T.]
- Garlic Cloves [1, Minced]
- Basil Leaves [.50 C.]

Directions

1. For this recipe, you will need a spiralizer. If you do not own one of these, you can buy zoodles or zucchini noodles in the produce section of your local grocery store. Once you have your zoodles, you are ready to get started.

2. The first step for this recipe will be heating a skillet over a moderate temperature. As it warms up, you will want to go ahead and sprinkle in some water and then add the zoodles. Once placed, cook the zucchini for eight minutes before adding in the cherry tomatoes, onion, and your minced garlic. When these items are in place, sauté for an additional five minutes.

3. When the zoodles are cooked to your liking, place into a mixing bowl with the white balsamic vinegar and coat evenly. At this point, you can portion your zoodles out and enjoy.

Gluten-Free Quinoa Pizza

Yield: [Six]

Prepping: [Thirty Minutes]

Ingredients

- Quinoa [1 C.]
- Baking Powder [1 t.]
- Coconut Oil [1 T.]
- Salt [Dash]
- Marinara Sauce [.25 C.]
- Plant-based Cheese [.25 C.]

Directions

1. Before you can make this incredible pizza, you will first need to prepare your quinoa. For best results, you will want to set the quinoa up the night before. When you do this, place the quinoa in a bowl and cover it with water. Once in place, allow the grain to soak overnight.

2. When you are set to make your pizza crust, you will want to prep the stove to 425. As this heats up, take the quinoa from the stove and drain the excess water. When you have completed this, go ahead and place it into your food processor along with the baking powder, a dash of salt, and a quarter cup of water.

3. Now that you have your pizza dough, it is time to pour the batter into a cake pan and smooth it out so that the top surface is even. Once it is ready, place the pan into the stove for fifteen minutes. After this time has passed, you will carefully want to flip the crust over and bake it for an additional five minutes.

4. With the crust created, remove the dish from the oven and allow it to sit for five minutes or so. Once cool enough to handle, you will next top with the marinara sauce and your plant-based cheese. At this point, feel free to season the dish however you deem fit.

5. When your pizza is perfect, pop the dish back into the oven for ten minutes and allow the plant-based cheese to melt completely. When the meal is cooked through, take it out of the stove and let it chill slightly before cutting and serving.

Curried Coconut Cauliflower

Yield: [Four]

Prepping: [One Hour]

Ingredients

- Coconut Milk [1 Can]
- Water [2 T.]
- Cauliflower [3 C.]
- Tomatoes [1 Can, Diced]
- Ginger [1 T.]
- Onion [1, Diced]
- Salt [Dash]
- Red Curry Paste [.25 C.]
- Jalapeno [1, Diced]

Directions

1. This dish offers a blend of flavors that are a little bit sweet and a little bit spicy. Whether you enjoy the cauliflower alone or on top of a bed of rice, this dish is sure to be a crowd-pleaser!

2. To start this recipe off, you will want to take out your large cooking pot and place it over a moderate temperature. As it warms up, add in some water and begin sautéing the jalapeno pepper and onion. After you have cooked these items for three minutes, stir in the curry paste and ginger.

3. Once you have sautéed these items for an additional minute, you can gently stir in the coconut milk and toss in the tomatoes. Finally, you will place in the cauliflower and take everything to a stew.

4. When you see bubbles, reduce the temperature and allow the Ingredients to simmer together for fifteen minutes. After that time has passed, take the pot away from the heat and portion out your dinner.

Simple Sticky Tofu

Yield: [Five]

Prepping: [Thirty Minutes]

Ingredients

- Extra-firm Tofu [1 Block, Cubed]
- Soy Sauce [1 T.]
- Hoisin Sauce [2 T.]
- Chives [1 T.]

Directions

1. Sometimes, your meal just needs some extra protein. While this tofu is on the simple side, it can be a great addition to any dish! You will want to start out by marinating the tofu in a mixture of the soy sauce, hoisin sauce, and the chives. If you like a bit of spice, try adding some red pepper flakes! Allow the tofu to soak for twenty minutes.

2. When you are ready to grill the tofu, take out your cooking pan and place over a moderate temperature. Once warm, add in the tofu and cook for five to ten minutes on each side. By the end, the tofu will be sticky and golden.

Basic Buddha Bowl

Yield: [Four]

Prepping: [One Hour]

Ingredients

- Quinoa [1 C.]
- Silken Tofu [1 Package]
- Sweet Potato [1, Cubed]
- Garlic Clove [3, Minced]
- Mushrooms [2 C., Sliced]
- Kale [3 C.]
- White Wine Vinegar [2 t.]
- Lemon Juice [2 t.]
- Salt [Dash]

Directions

1. For a dish that is both sweet, savory, and packed with vegetables, this recipe has got it all! To begin this basic buddha bowl, go ahead and prep the stove to 425.

2. As the stove heats up, you will want to cook the quinoa according to the Directions provided on the package. Once it is fluffy and cooked through, remove from your stovetop and set to the side.

3. Next, it is time to cook your sweet potato! Once the oven is heated up, you will want to dice the sweet potato up into bite-sized pieces and place on a cooking sheet. After you have seasoned the pieces to your liking, roast it in the oven for fifteen minutes. When this time has passed, the sweet potato should be soft and cooked through.

4. Now it is time to make the mushrooms and the kale! To complete this step, get out a skillet and begin heating it over a moderate temperature. Once warm, add in the kale with the garlic and stir for ten minutes or so. After the kale begins to wilt, add in the mushrooms and cook for an additional ten minutes.

5. The last step of creating this buddha bowl will be creating your sauce! For this step, you'll need your food processor. Once out, add in the lemon juice, a clove of garlic, white vinegar, and the tofu. As you blend everything out, you may need to throw in some water to make the sauce less thick.

6. Now that all of the items are prepared, you will want to start with a base of quinoa and top with the rest of the Ingredients. Finally, drizzle the sauce over the top of everything, and dinner is all set!

Plant-Based Shepherd's Pie

Yield: [Six]

Prepping: [One Hour]

Ingredients

- Vegetable Stock [4 C.]
- Lentils [2 C.]
- Garlic Clove [1, Minced]
- Onion [1, Diced]
- Salt [Dash]
- Mixed Vegetables [1 Can]
- Potatoes [10]
- Plant-based Butter {2 T.]
- Pepper [Dash]

Directions

1. Plant-based or not, Shepherd's pie is a classic dinner meal! To start this recipe off, you will first want to boil your potatoes. You can complete this task the way you usually would. Just boil them for thirty minutes and then set to the side.

2. Once the potatoes are cooked nice and soft, you will want to place them into a mixing bowl and begin smashing down with your potato masher until they are nice and smooth. If you would like, add some plant-based butter and season to your liking.

3. Next, go ahead and heat your stove to 425. As it warms up, you will also want to get out your baking dish and line it with some parchment paper.

4. As these prepare for the recipe, the next step to take will be getting out a cooking pan and placing it over a moderate heat. As it warms, add in some water and the onions. You will cook these for five minutes before adding in your vegetable stock and lentils. When the Ingredients begin to boil, turn the temperature down and allow lentils to simmer for forty minutes.

5. In the last ten minutes of the lentils cooking, you can add in your mixed vegetables. If you like a thicker shepherd's pie, add in a couple of tablespoons of cornstarch!

6. When these Ingredients are cooked through, you will carefully pour them into the bottom of your baking dish. Once in place, cover with the mashed potatoes you made in the second step and season to your liking. When the dish is set, place it into the oven for fifteen minutes.

7. By the end, the top should be browned, and your shepherd's pie is complete for dinner!

CHAPTER 7:

Desserts

Coconut Dessert Balls

Yield: [Twelve]

Prepping: [Forty Minutes]

Ingredients

- Unsweetened Coconut Milk [2 T.]
- Coconut Oil [2 t.]
- Shredded Coconut [2 C.]
- Salt [Dash]
- Ground Cinnamon [.50 t.]
- Vanilla Extract [1 t.]
- Maple Syrup [3 T.]

Directions

1. If you are a fan of coconut, you will definitely want to test out this dessert. They are easy to make and easy to grab when you need something sweet. To start out, you are going to take only one cup of your shredded coconut and put it into your food processor with the melted coconut oil. Go ahead and mend everything together until you get a paste.

2. When the first step is complete, you will also want to place the salt, cinnamon, vanilla, coconut milk, and the maple syrup in. You can also add another couple of tablespoons of coconut in and pulse again.

3. Now that you have your dough, y0u will want to use your hands to roll balls. Generally, you should be able to make between ten and twelve balls. Once they are set, carefully roll and press them into your remaining shredded coconut.

4. When you are finished, you'll want to pop the balls into the fridge for at least an hour before consuming it. After this, you are set to enjoy your dessert.

Sweet Chia Pudding

Yield: [Two]

Prepping: [Five Minutes]

Ingredients

- Chia Seeds [2 T.]
- Medjool Dates [4}
- Cacao Powder [2 T.]
- Vanilla Extract [.25 t.]
- Unsweetened Almond Milk [1 C.]

Directions

1. When people think of chia seeds, they often don't feel they belong in a dessert. I challenge you to let this recipe change your mind! To start out, you are going to want to take all of the items from the list above and put them into your food processor.

2. When everything is smooth together, you will want to stop several times to scrape down the sides. If needed, you can add more or less cacao powder depending on your own taste. If you like your pudding on the sweeter side, you will want to consider adding more dates as well.

3. Last but not least, pour the pudding into your serving bowls and pop into the fridge for thirty minutes. After this, the pudding should be chilled and will be ready for dessert.

Cinnamon Apple Pie

Yield: [Eight]

Prepping: [Three Hours]

Ingredients

- Apples [6 C., Sliced]
- Pre-made Pie Crust [1 Package]
- Ground Nutmeg [.10 t.]
- Sugar [1 C.]
- Salt [Dash]
- Ground Cinnamon [1 t.]
- Lemon Juice [1 T.]
- All-purpose Flour [2 T.]

Directions

1. While this pie does take around three hours to make, there must be time spent on making the perfect apple pie! This pie will have your guests coming back for seconds and even thirds! When you are all set, go ahead and prep the stove to 425. As this warms up, you can take out your pie crust and press it into a glass pie dish.

2. Next, it is time to prep your apples! With each apple, you will want to core and peel before doing anything else. Once you have completed this, you will want to slice the apples up thin and place them into your mixing bowl.

3. When your apples are in place, go ahead and add in the rest of the items from the list above. Be sure to mend everything together well to spread the flavors out evenly. Once the filling has been created, spoon it gently into your pie plate and smooth out.

4. Now that your filling is in place, carefully top the second crust over the top and wrap any excess under the bottom of the lower crust. You will want to take a few moments here to really press the edges together, so you create a nice seal on your pie. When this is complete, cut some slits on the top of your pie for ventilation.

5. With your pie all set, it is time to get to the baking! If your oven is heated to the correct temperature, pop the dish into the stove for forty-five minutes. During the last five minutes, you will want to keep a close eye on the pie to make sure it isn't burning.

6. If you don't like a crispy crust, you will want to cover the edges of y0ur pie with tin foil during the first twenty minutes of baking your pie. You will only need a three-inch strip of foil to wrap around the whole pie.

7. When your crust is a golden color, remove the pie from the oven and place it onto your cooling rack. Once here, you will want to leave the pie out for two hours before you slice and serve!

Blueberry and Lemon Cheesecake

Yield: [Four]

Prepping: [One Hour]

Ingredients

- Coconut Oil [2 T.]
- Maple Syrup [.25 C.]
- Vanilla Bean Powder [.50 t.]
- Pecans [2 C.]
- Coconut Oil [1.25 C.]
- Maple Syrup [.75 C.]
- Cashews [3 C.]
- Lemon Juice [1.50 C.]
- Coconut Oil [1 T.]
- Maple Syrup [1 T.]
- Blueberries [1 C.]

Directions

1. Cheesecake is a dessert classic! While you on the plant-based diet, you won't be eating the traditional cheesecake, but there is nothing stopping you from making your own! This recipe does take several steps, but it is worth the work!

2.   The very first step of this recipe is going to make making your crust! For this, you will want to get out your food processor and mend together the vanilla bean powder with the melted coconut oil, pecans, and the maple syrup. Go ahead and blend these on high until you get a sticky and crumbly texture. When this is set, place it into your baking dish and spread it along the bottom.

3.   Next, it is time to make the cheesecake! For this step, you will want to soak your cashews for at least thirty minutes before this recipe. When they are soft, drain the water out and place it into your food processor. Once here, also add in your one and a quarter cups of coconut oil along with the maple syrup and the lemon juice. You will want to process on high until smooth. When this is set, pour it into your baking dish and spread across the surface of your crust.

4.   Last, but not least, it is time to make the blueberry swirl topping! For this, you'll just need a tablespoon of your coconut oil, a tablespoon of the maple syrup, and the blueberries. When this becomes smooth in the food processor, carefully drizzle it across your cheesecake mixture. Get creative!

5.   Now that your cheesecake it all set, you are going to want to pop the dish into your freezer for at least three hours. By the end of this time, your cheesecake should be firm! If you are looking to serve the dessert soon, you will want to remove from the freezer for ten minutes before slicing and serving.

Yield: [Four]

Prepping: [Twenty Minutes]

Ingredients

- Old-fashioned Oats [2 T.]
- Flour [1 t.]
- Flour [3 t.]
- Cinnamon [.50 t.]
- Peaches [2]
- Coconut Oil [3 t.]
- Brown Sugar [2 T.]
- Sugar [1 t.]

Directions

1. If you need a quick dessert for two, this recipe is easy to make but still packs some flavor! You will want to begin by prepping your stove to 375. If you have small baking dishes or two ramekins, you will want to get them out and line them with parchment paper.

2. Next, it is time to make the filling for your peach cobbler. For this, you will want to start out by peeling your peaches and dicing them into bite-sized pieces. Once this is complete, place them into a mixing bowl along with the sugar, cinnamon, and flour. Be sure to toss so the flavors spread evenly.

3. In another bowl, it is time to make the crumble top. For this, you will just have to mend the flour, oats, and brown sugar. When this is complete, you can also add in your coconut oil and clump everything together.

4. When you are set to make your dessert, you will first lay in the peach mixture into the bottom of your dishes and carefully layer the crumble top over the peaches.

5. Next, you'll want to pop the dishes into the stove for about fifteen minutes. By the end, the crumble top will be golden, and your peaches should be slightly bubbling.

6. When your dessert is cooked through, remove from the stove, and enjoy your sweet treat!

Baked Cinnamon Apples

Yield: [Four]

Prepping: [Forty Minutes]

Ingredients

- Cinnamon [2 t.]
- Brown Sugar [.25 C.]
- Apples [2 Lbs.]
- Lemon [1]

Directions

1. While on the plant-based diet, you will be amazed at how simple a dessert can be but still delicious. Many people feel that desserts need to be packed with sugar and calories in order to taste good, but that simply is not the case! As you can see, this recipe only requires four Ingredients, and it is still delicious. To begin this recipe, prep your stove to 375.

2. As the stove heats up, you will want to take a few moments to prep your apples. The best way to do this will be by coring each apple, peeling, and chopping them into bite-sized pieces. For this recipe, I suggest using either gala apples or Cortland apples.

3. Next, you will want to take your mixing bowl out so that you can combine the apples with the lemon juice, cinnamon, and brown sugar. For this recipe, feel free to adjust the flavors to your own taste. Once the apples are coated, place them into a casserole dish.

4. Now, you will want to cook the apples in the stove for about thirty minutes. For even cooking, you will want to stir the apples around a couple of times during the baking process. By the end, the apples should appear to be juicy and soft. If they look cooked through, take the dish away from the oven and set out to chill for a few minutes.

5. Finally, you can enjoy these apples as a dessert or as a sweet side!

Sweet Snickerdoodle Snack

Yield: [Twenty]

Prepping: [One Hour]

Ingredients

- Medjool Dates [1.50 C.]
- Ground Cinnamon [2 t.]
- Vanilla Extract [.25 t.]
- Salt [Dash]
- Cashews [1 C.]
- Almonds [1 C.]

Directions

1. If you are someone who is always on the go, you will want to consider a dessert that you can grab and pack when you need it. You never know when those sugar cravings are going to hit, and it is better to be prepared than to break your diet! As you can tell, this recipe has very simple Ingredients but will still hit the spot!

2. The first step of this recipe will be placing the almonds and cashews into your food processor and blending until the nuts become very fine. When they are more like a powder, add in your cinnamon, salt, vanilla extract, and your dates. As you blend these items together, you will notice a sticky dough forming.

3. When the dough reaches the proper consistency, you will want to use your hands to begin rolling balls. Generally, this recipe should be able to make about twenty, bite-sized snack balls. When these are set, you will want to pop them into the fridge for an hour before digging in.

Plant-Based Peanut Butter Cookies

Yield: [Ten]

Prepping: [Thirty Minutes]

Ingredients

- Peanut Butter [2 T.]
- Banana [1, Sliced]
- Coconut Flour [.25 C.]
- Vanilla Extract [.50 t.]

Directions

1. Whether you want to bake a batch of cookies for yourself or if you need something to bring to an event, these peanut butter and banana cookies are tasty and healthy at the same time! When you are set to begin cooking, you will first want to prep the stove to 350.

2. As the stove heats up, get out your mixing bowl and mash together the vanilla extract, peanut butter, and the banana. When these are mended well, add in the coconut flour as well. Note that if you like your cookies on the sweeter side, feel free to add in some sweetener of your choice.

3. Now that you have your dough use your hands to roll small balls and place them onto a baking sheet. Once in place, you will want to slightly flatten the cookies out and use a fork to create crisscross shapes into your cookies.

4. When you are set, pop the dish into the stove for about fifteen minutes. By the end of this time, the cookies will begin to crisp around the edges and turn golden.

5. Once the cookies are cooked to your liking, remove from the oven and permit them to chill for at least five minutes before serving.

CHAPTER 8:

Creating Your Own Meal Plan

While having a wide selection of recipes to choose from can be helpful when you are starting a new diet, you may have no clue what to do with these recipes. For this reason, you will want to come up with a meal plan!

When you create a meal plan, it may seem overwhelming at first if you have never done this before. The good news is that with practice, you will be a planning pro before you know it. When creating your meal plans, there is no reason to go wild and crazy. I highly suggest starting out with just a day or two before graduating onto planning for the week.

With meal plans, you will want to create a plan that is based around your specific needs. At the end of this book, you will find a meal plan that was created to help the general public. With that being said, the guide in this book is meant to help beginners learn how to follow a plant-based diet on a regular basis. Below, you will find some of my favorite tips and tricks to creating your own meal plans that are custom-tailored to your lifestyle.

Step One: Find Your Number

The first step you are going to take when creating your meal plans will be determining how many mouths you are going to be feeding. If you are feeding a family, meal planning can become slightly more difficult. We all have different tastes, so it can be hard finding meals that everyone is going to like, especially if they are not used to eating plant-based. If you have never meal prepped before, you may want to consider just planning for yourself at first. This can give you good practice before you start planning multiple servings.

While this may seem like it shouldn't be such a big deal, meal planning can change in a number of different ways when you are cooking for several people under your roof. It is absolutely manageable, but you will want to keep in consideration how much food you will have to purchase when you are planning for the week.

Step Two: Budget, Budget, Budget

Once you have determined how many people you are going to be cooking for, you will next want to take a look at your budget. While following a plant-based diet, you may notice that it can be a tad bit more expensive when shopping fresh produce compared to the processed junk you're used to buying. If you are on a tight budget, there are plenty of ways to work a plant-based diet into the said budget. Whether you buy frozen or per season, there are plenty of ways to take advantage of a healthier diet.

If you haven't thought about your food budget, you may want to start keeping a record of what you are spending on food. This is where the first step comes in hand. Obviously, if you are shopping for one, you are going to be able to afford more Ingredients compared to shopping for a whole family. If you are shopping for a whole family, consider adding recipes to your meal plan that uses some of the same Ingredients or incorporate leftovers!

Step Three: Cooking Time Budget

While having a meal plan is fine and dandy, I want you to take a step back and really think about how much time you are going to want to spend in the kitchen. If you aren't a fan of cooking, unfortunately, a meal plan isn't going to become more enjoyable just because you have created a plan.

As a beginner, you may want to consider keeping your meals as simple as possible. There is nothing wrong with whipping together a simple salad or sandwich if you don't feel like cooking! Especially in the beginning, you may not want to spend that much time in the kitchen when you are first starting out. You may want to consider purchasing an Instant Pot or Slow cooker to do some of the heavy work for you.

Step Four: Motivation and Goals

Before you even think about creating your meal plan for the week, you need to take a good look in the mirror and ask yourself why are you doing this in the first place? What is the reason we do anything?

As you create your meal plan, you will want to keep your goals in mind. Are you looking to lose weight? Do you want to be healthy? Do you just want to eat at least one, plant-based meal to kickstart your journey? Whatever your goal is, keep it in mind as you begin thinking about meals you will be enjoying for the week.

Step Five: Get to Planning

Now that you have fully prepared for the week, it is time to get planning. While it may seem silly to incorporate all of these different variables for a silly meal plan, it is going to save you a lot of time and stress at the grocery store. When you have a plan, you know exactly what you need and exactly how much time it is going to take you.

If you are a busy person, I suggest taking some time during Saturday or Sunday to write out your meal plan, hit the grocery store, and even prep a few meals for the week. If you have gone through the recipes from the chapters above, you can see that many of these meals are meant to be prepared ahead of time for when you are on the go.

When you are creating your plan, I suggest keeping breakfast and lunch fairly simple. You can pre-make some breakfast cookies or a smoothie for breakfast and enjoy a simple salad for lunch. There is no shame in keeping your meals simple, as long as you remain plant-based along the way.

As you will see in the meal plan provided in this book, that is the way it is going to be set up for the first couple of weeks. Your focus can be on prepping dinner meals for the week. The best news is, if you are only cooking for one or two people, you will have an instant lunch the next day!

Whether you are planning three meals, six meals, or even twelve meals, you will eventually get the hang of it. During the first few weeks of figuring out meal prep, remember to be kind to yourself. We all hit some bumps along the way, and some food may accidentally go to waste, but it is not in vain. Eventually, you will know exactly how much food you need, and you'll learn how to combine Ingredients to create several types of recipes.

With all of that in mind, it is time to jump into the three-week kick start! Here, you will find everything you need to know to help you get started on your new, plant-based diet. From my favorite tips and tricks to learning how to follow my specific meal plan, you will be ready to get started before you know it!

CHAPTER 9:

Starting the 3-Week Kick-Start

Before we jump into the meal plan, I want to take a moment to congratulate you on choosing to start this journey. You are probably already aware that the plant-based diet is going to be able to bring you a number of benefits, but there is something special about experiencing these benefits for yourself rather than just hearing about them.

Once upon a time, there may have been a point where you have asked yourself if you got your servings of vegetables in for the day. From this point on, the mass majority of your diet is going to be vegetables, so you will never have to worry about that again!

If you are excited to get started, but you feel overwhelmed by the thought, I hope that you will utilize the following three-week kick-start guide to help you get started. Within this meal plan, you will find some of my favorite plant-based recipes to help you get started on your own health journey.

Before we begin, I also wanted to provide you with some of my top tips and tricks of getting started on a plant-based diet. By implementing these tricks, you will find it easier, starting a new lifestyle. As you practice plant-based more, it will become like second nature to you without you even realizing it.

Tips and Tricks of Eating Plant-based

Clean the Pantry

From this point on, I want you to look at this day as day number one! There is no looking back and no turning around from this point. The best tip I can provide you is cleaning out your pantry and your fridge as soon as possible. Whether you recycle, toss, or donate, just get rid of the non-compliant items! You will want to get rid of anything from white bread, deli meats, dairy products, processed foods, and sugary drinks. When you get rid of the bad, you will be making room for the good.

Create Your Meal Plan

In this case, you will be following mine at first. If you feel that the meal plan provided is not fit for your lifestyle, use the chapter from above to make your own plan! As you plan out your meals, this will help you restock your fridge and pantry, now that you have gotten rid of all the unhealthy items.

As you practice the plant-based diet for a longer period of time, you will learn some of your favorite staples to keep in stock. Remember that there is no reason to make your diet more complicated than it needs to be. Some popular staples will be fresh fruits and vegetables, oats, beans, and seeds.

Spend Time Finding Recipes

When you are first starting a plant-based diet, it is going to be important that you go in with a plan! The best way to do this will be spending some time on the internet (or this book), finding some plant-based recipes that you want to try.

If you are having a hard time thinking about meals you want to try, the easiest way to find recipes is to start with foods that you enjoy. As you do more research, you will find that there are a number of different ways to make your favorite recipes as a plant-based version. Whether you like burgers, mac, and cheese, or tacos, there is a plant-based recipe for those.

Find Your Motivation

Much like with everything in life, there is no point in doing anything if you have no motivation to do so. If you are just starting out, I suggest getting out a piece of paper or an index card and write down your why. While it may seem silly, it can be helpful to have a visual of your goals for the plant-based diet. If you are able to see it on a daily basis, this will act as your motivation to make healthier food choices throughout the week.

Slow Down Shopping

As you begin the plant-based diet, you may be surprised to learn some of the foods that you never thought about purchasing before. Often times when we get to the grocery store, we want to be in and out so that we can get home, but now, I suggest you slow down and spend some extra time in the grocery store.

Now that you are eating more whole foods, it will be important that you are selecting produce that is going to benefit you. As you stroll through the produce section, spend even just an extra ten minutes checking out Ingredients such as tempeh, quinoa, and different plant-based milks for you to try. As you expand your horizons, you never know what will become a new favorite in your diet!

Simple Salads

When you are first starting a plant-based diet, it is all too easy to become overly eager to get to planning intense meals for the week.

If you feel this way, I want to make sure you understand that it is perfectly okay to keep your meals simple! For this reason, I highly suggest you incorporate eating a salad on a daily basis.

When you are eating salad, this is a perfect way to get in a couple of servings of vegetables and even a serving of fruit! As you plan grocery shopping for the week, choose some salad bar choices to keep the salads fresh and exciting. Salads are easy to whip together and can be transported on the go when you need a healthy lunch at work or on the road.

Meatless Monday

One of the top struggles people have when first starting the plant-based diet is giving up meat for good. If you are among these individuals, I suggest testing out Meatless Monday! For this, you will want to pick out one recipe for Monday that normally has meat but remove the meat from the recipe! As you begin to practice this on a daily basis, you can begin incorporating a meatless day throughout your week until, eventually, you are completely plant-based.

Another way to practice meatless days is to choose one meal that you are going to eat without meat. Whether this is breakfast or lunch, you will want to be conscious of this decision. Luckily, there are plenty of recipes out there that require no meat and will help make the transition to plant-based much easier rather just cutting meat out cold turkey. (Get it??)

Focus on the Positive

Last, but not least, I want you to think of this lifestyle change as a good thing. One of the main reasons people fail their diet is because they become so focused on what they are "missing out on." If possible, I want you to focus on what you can enjoy on your new diet, rather than what you are not eating. On a plant-based diet, there is a variety of fresh produce for you to try and enjoy. It is going to take some extra work, but as your palette changes and you kick your sugar addiction, you will wonder why you haven't been eating like this your whole life!

Getting Started on the Kick-Start

Before diving into the meal plan (though I know you are extremely excited,) there are several steps that you will want to take before you dive right in.

In the three chapters to follow, you will see that I have broken down your meal plan into three weeks and day by day. If you see a recipe that you are not a fan of, feel free to swap it out with any other recipe provided in this book! The point of following the meal plan is to make the transition period easier for you. By the end of the three weeks, I hope you will feel confident in your skills to begin meal planning all by yourself.

For the meal plan provided in this book, I will also be providing you with a grocery list. If you plan on changing anything, be sure that you change your grocery list as well. I highly suggest grouping your Ingredients together, depending on the departments in your grocery store. This way, you can save yourself time from searching through the list and hitting all different sections of your store. The good news is that a majority of your Ingredients are going to be coming from the perimeter of the store.

Speaking of saving time, another time-saving tip you will want to consider is saving the day for meal prep! When you are picking out your recipes, you will want to consider just prepping for the week. This way, you are finishing your cooking on a day that you have energy, and then you will have meals for you to grab and go. My favorite day to shop and prep is on Sunday because I am off from work, and I have time to focus on my nutrition.

Another way to save time during your prepping will be chopping up your vegetables for the week. By doing this, they will be prepared for when you are cooking during the week or can serve as a quick and easy snack! Either way, you will want to consider prepping at the beginning of the week to save yourself time later!

Now that I have said enough, it is time to jump into the meal plan! As I said earlier, the meal plan to follow is meant for the general population. It is going to help you learn the foods you will be enjoying on a plant-based diet rather than struggling to try to determine for yourself. If you feel ready to begin your health journey, let's jump right in! If you have any questions, the chapter after will provide you with some more tips and tricks to help you get started.

CHAPTER 10:

Week One

Congratulations on starting week one of your kick-start meal plan! As you follow along with the meal plan, remember that there is no reason to stay rigid! As you begin the plant-based diet, you shouldn't expect yourself to be an expert overnight. Learning how to change your diet and lifestyle is going to take time and practice.

Before we get started, there is a list of kitchen tools you will want to consider. While they aren't necessarily needed for the following recipes, they work wonders with saving you time during the cooking process.

Cooking Essentials

Blender/Food Processor

When it comes to saving time, it is important to have a good blender or food processor on time. With an excellent blender that has sharp blades, you will be able to make anything from smoothies to soups to ice cream with little to no effort. A food processor is a little less necessary, but they are great to have on hands when you are working with seeds and nuts. As you may have noticed, a number of recipes included in this book require one of the other.

Baking Dishes/Tray

A lot of people fail to realize how important it is to have the proper cooking equipment. When you first begin the plant-based diet, you will find that you are going to be doing a lot more cooking now. For this reason, I highly suggest investing in some heavy-duty baking trays and dishes. It will make your life a lot easier when you have the proper equipment on hand!

Silicone Baking Mat or Parchment Paper

Speaking of saving time, who really enjoys cleaning the dishes after working so hard on the cooking portion of the meal? To help keep cooking clean and quick, you'll want to invest in silicone baking mats or parchment paper. This will save at least one dish from having to be cleaned!

Knives

I cannot express how important sharp knives are when it comes to cooking. As you incorporate more fresh produce into your plant-based diet, you can expect to be doing a lot of chopping, mincing, and dicing. When you have dull knives, there is nothing more frustrating than trying to chop through hard vegetables and not being able to. I suggest having one big knife to do a majority of your chopping, but it is always good to have a few medium knives on hand for smaller slicing.

Proper Storage Containers

Last but not least, the key behind successful meal prep is going to be proper storage containers. This way, you do the cooking, place them into their container, and then all you will have to do is grab and go! It saves you time, saves you space, and stops you from wasting food! It is a win-win situation!

Now that you have your essential items! Let's get started on Week One!

Week One Outline

Monday	Tuesday	Wednesday	Thursday	Friday	Saturday
Chia Seed Breakfast Bowl	Fruit Smoothie	Chia Seed Breakfast Bowl	Fruit Smoothie	Chia Seed Breakfast Bowl	Carrot Pancakes
Salad	Leftovers or Salad	Leftovers or Salad	Leftovers or Salad	Leftovers or Salad	Leftovers or Salad
Spiced Chickpea Stew	TBD	Simple Sticky Tofu	TBD	Spicy 'Chicken' Wraps	TBD

Shopping List

Fruits

- ➢ Blueberries
- ➢ Banana
- ➢ Tomato
- ➢ Lemon Juice

Vegetables

- ➢ Kale
- ➢ Green Chilies
- ➢ Chives
- ➢ Mixed Greens

<u>Cooking Items/Spices</u>

- ➤ Chia Seeds
- ➤ Peanut Butter
- ➤ Coffee
- ➤ Rolled Oats
- ➤ Whole Wheat Wraps
- ➤ Cashews
- ➤ Hot Sauce
- ➤ Apple Cider Vinegar
- ➤ Chickpeas
- ➤ Soy Sauce
- ➤ Hoisin Sauce
- ➤ Extra-firm Tofu

<u>Spices</u>

- ➤ Dried Parsley
- ➤ Dried Dill
- ➤ Garlic Cloves
- ➤ Coriander Leaves

<u>Plant-based Dairy</u>

- ➤ Almond Milk

Since this is your first week following a meal plan, I highly suggest that you choose one day to do your grocery shopping and prepping for the week. Many people choose to do this on Sunday, but you can go shopping on any day that you have more time.

As soon as you get home, you will want to wash all of your fresh produce. If you have the time, you can prep the fruits and vegetables and place them into your food containers. This way, if you don't plan on doing any cooking until the day of, the Ingredients will already be prepped for you!

During the first week, I want you to learn how to be comfortable with the Ingredients that you will be able to enjoy on your new diet. As you can tell from the overview, I have only included a handful of recipes for you to plan for the week. For the rest of the meals, it is okay to be slightly more relaxed on your diet. Of course, I suggest that you also make these meals as plant-based as possible, but we are not striving for perfection here.

Perfection is a common trap that many people fall into. The issue is, if you get too down on yourself, there is no way that you will stick to the plan! As long as you are 75% plant-based during this first week, consider it a win! A good way to accomplish this will be following the meal plan and only focusing on one or two meals throughout the week.

Breakfast

For breakfast, you will find two separate recipes. The first recipe is the chia seed breakfast bowl. This is a great first recipe as you are starting a plant-based diet because it is simple to make and will only take about fifteen minutes. For the other day, all you will need is your favorite fruit and a cup of plant-based milk. You may be surprised just how filling a fruit smoothie can be! As you become more comfortable with plant-based Ingredients, you can get extremely fancy with your morning smoothies!

Lunch

During your first week on the plant-based diet, I don't want you to worry too much about lunch. As mentioned earlier, there is no shame in keeping a meal extremely simple. For lunch this week, I challenge you to have a salad every day. Whether you create your own or use one of the recipes included in this book, aim for a salad for lunch. If you lack the Ingredients, you can always enjoy your leftovers from dinner the night before. This is a great way to save time and money!

Dinner

Last but not least, we have dinner for the week. During the first week of your diet, it can seem very overwhelming. If it helps, you can choose to just focus on dinner recipes for the week. Remember that we are striving for progress, not perfection! For this first week, I wanted to introduce three different yet simple recipes for you to try. Between the chickpea stew, sticky tofu, and 'chicken' wraps, you will find a variety of flavors and textures to give you a good introduction to plant-based foods. If you find this too overwhelming, feel free to only try one or two of the recipes this week!

This is your journey; you are the only one who knows how much cooking you can handle.

Before you jump into week two, you may notice that I have not included snacks or dessert during this first week, and that is for a very good reason.

If you are looking to lose weight while following a plant-based diet, you are going to have to learn how to limit your calories. The best way to do this will be by focusing on your nutrition in your meals and cutting down on any unnecessary snacking.

As you become more comfortable on your plant-based diet, you can absolutely begin to incorporate snacking and dessert, but this is the first week of changing over your eating habits. Our main focus for this week is increasing plant-based items and slowly getting rid of meat and processed items. In the last week or so, you will find some snack and dessert recipes for you to enjoy.

If you are set, get your grocery list set, and you are ready to go!

CHAPTER 11:

Week Two

Can you believe you have made it through week one already? Congratulations!

Before we move onto week two, take a few moments to reflect on week one. Where did you excel? Where did you feel like you failed? Did you follow the meal plan as much as you would have liked?

Starting any diet can be extremely difficult. Up until this point, you are probably used to a certain style of eating and the same old eating schedule. As you begin following a meal plan, you probably find that you don't have as much time to cook as you thought. This is especially true for those of us who work all day and simply don't have the energy to cook at the end of the day. For this reason, I am going to introduce meal prepping this week.

Hopefully, at this point, you are feeling slightly more comfortable with the items you are able to enjoy on the plant-based diet. If you are feeling comfortable, I invite you to challenge yourself to meal prep. You had a good head start getting used to shopping and prepping the vegetables in the first week, so we are just going to take that one step further.

For purposes of learning how to meal prep, we are going to limit the meals for the week once again. For the other meals labeled TBD, keep the meals as simple as possible. Whether the meal is a salad or leftovers, your goal for this week should be incorporating more plant-based meals. If you haven't given up the meat or the dairy yet, that is perfectly okay! Slow and steady wins the race. Remember, the sooner you make the switch, the sooner you get the benefits from the healthy foods! Your success is completely in your hands; it is all about making the best possible choice for yourself.

Week Two Overview

Monday	Tuesday	Wednesday	Thursday	Friday	Saturday	Sunday
Plant-based Muffins	Fruit Smoothie	Plant-based Muffins	Fruit Smoothie	Plant-based Muffins	Carrot Pancakes	Fruit Smoothie
Build Your Own Salad	Build Your Own Salad	Build Your Own Salad	Build Your Own Salad	Build Your Own Salad	Build Your Own Salad	Build Your Own Salad
Lentil and Butternut Squash Soup	Plant-based Shepherd Pie	Lentil and Butternut Squash Soup	Basic Buddha Bowl	Lentil and Butternut Squash Soup	Basic Buddha Bowl	Leftovers from any Dinner

Shopping List

<u>Fruits</u>

➢ Blueberries

➢ Banana

➢ Apples

<u>Vegetables</u>

➢ Carrots

➢ Lentils

- Mixed Greens
- Spinach
- Butternut Squash
- Onion
- Mixed Vegetables
- Potatoes
- Sweet Potatoes
- Mushrooms
- Kale

Cooking Items

- Old Fashioned Oats
- Chopped Walnuts
- Pancake Mix
- Vegetable Broth
- Quinoa
- Silken Tofu
- White Wine Vinegar
- Lemon Juice

Spices

- Ground Cloves
- Cinnamon
- Nutmeg
- Garlic Cloves
- Fresh Ginger

➢ Cayenne Pepper

➢ Curry Powder

Plant-based Dairy

➢ Almond Milk

➢ Plant-based Butter

While this shopping list is a bit longer, you should not let that intimidate you! The good news is that this week, you are going to prep most of these recipes on one day. If you have time, I suggest shopping and cooking on the same day. By doing your meal plan this way, you can get the hard work out of the way and enjoy the fruits of your labor for the rest of the week!

Breakfast

For your second week on the plant-based diet, I have set up three different breakfast choices, including plant-based breakfast muffins, a fruit smoothie, and delicious carrot pancakes as a treat!

I wanted to include these particular recipes because they are easy to meal prep in the beginning of the week and have only a handful of Ingredients for you to purchase. For the plant-based muffins, the recipe yields six muffins, meaning you could have enough for the week if you are not splitting with other people. If you can, prep this recipe to use for several days. To provide an alternative choice, you can also prep the carrot pancakes for the week!

Lunch

For lunch, we are going to continue to build salad for this meal. I wanted to include daily salads on your three-week kick-start because it is an easy way to get a serving of protein and vegetables into your daily macros. While many people think they need to eat plain salad in order to be "healthy," there are plenty of ways of building a great salad.

Building a Super Salad

➤ Base

When you are building your salad, the most essential part is going to be your base! Instead of choosing iceberg lettuce, which offers very little nutritional value, you will want to consider a green such as romaine lettuce, spring mix, or kale.

➤ Make it Colorful

Once your base is all set, you will want to throw on as many vegetables as you want! Some excellent choices include tomatoes, carrots, bell peppers, radishes, mushrooms, and the list goes on! To save yourself some time, consider chopping these vegetables up at the beginning of the week, so you just have to toss and eat.

➤ Healthy Fats

Unfortunately, fat has a really bad reputation. As you begin the plant-based diet, it will be important that you learn the difference between healthy fats and unhealthy fats. Some great choices to consider for your salads include olives, seeds, nuts, and avocados. These offer alternative flavors and textures as you build different salads.

➤ Protein

Last but not least, we have protein to add to your perfect salad. By adding protein, this can create a balanced meal that will keep you filled and satisfied. Many people think that the only protein for salad is chicken or steak, but on the plant-based diet, beans are going to be your best friend! Some popular choices include chickpeas, black beans, and kidney beans!

Dinner

As far as dinner goes during this second week, you will be in charge of preparing three different meals. The first recipe, Lentil & Butternut

Squash Soup, can be prepared on Sunday night. Soups and stews are always beneficial for meal prepping during a busy week because you can make larger batches of these recipes. For this first week of practicing meal prep., you will want to try to portion this soup out to the last three meals.

On the other days, you have plant-based shepherd's pie and the basic Buddha Bowl. Please note that the point of a buddha bowl is to be completely customizable. The recipe provided in this book includes silken tofu, mushrooms, sweet potato, and quinoa. If you like another vegetable, feel free to add it in too! If you have any leftovers from dinner, feel free to have them as lunch instead of building a salad.

Snacks

As you move into week two, you will get a better feel on your hunger levels. One of the major benefits people notice on the plant-based diet is how filling eating whole foods can be. If you still feel you need to snack on your new diet, it is better to have a healthy snack on hand rather than reaching for something unhealthy and processed. I suggest trying one of the following recipes included in this book:

- ➤ Basic Energy Snack Bars
- ➤ Pizza Quinoa Snack Balls
- ➤ Cheese Kale Bites
- ➤ Easy Baked Carrot Chips

Just like that, you will be moving through your second week on the plant-based diet like a champ! If there are any other recipes in this book that sparked your interest, feel free to add them into your week plan wherever you deem fit!

CHAPTER 12:

Week Three

When we first begin the plant-based diet, the first couple of weeks feel fairly easily. We are fueled by our motivation and our dreams of reaching our fitness goals. As you begin week three, you may find the excitement of your new diet begin to fade; and that is perfectly normal!

In the chapter to follow, you will find some of my best-kept secrets of sticking to any diet plan you choose to follow. What you may not know is that we are creatures of habit. We crave a routine to follow, and by learning how to find a routine with your diet, you will create higher chances of sticking to your diet in the first place.

Our goal for the third week is to find a routine that you will enjoy following. There should be no point in your plant-based diet that you feel you are being tortured by your diet. Instead, look at your food choices in a positive light! You are able to appreciate and enjoy fresh foods that are fueling you with nutrients. Plus, this week, we introduce dessert!

Week Three Overview

Monday	Tuesday	Wednesday	Thursday	Friday	Saturday	Sunday
Superfood Breakfast Bowl	Fruit Smoothie	Superfood Breakfast Bowl	Fruit Smoothie	Superfood Breakfast Bowl	Fruit Smoothie	Plant-based French Toast
Classic Kale Salad	Dinner Leftovers or Classic Kale Salad	Dinner Leftovers or Quick and Easy Chickpea Soup	Dinner Leftovers or Quick and Easy Chickpea Soup	Dinner Leftovers or Loaded Plant-based Nachos	Dinner Leftovers or Creamed Cauliflower Soup	Dinner Leftovers or Creamed Cauliflower Soup
Fried Thai Quinoa or Salad	Build Your Own Salad	Simple Sticky Tofu	Build Your Own Salad	Simple Sticky Tofu	Build Your Own Salad	Basic Buddha Bowl

Shopping List

Fruits

- ➢ Blueberries
- ➢ Mulberries
- ➢ Goji Berries

Vegetables

- ➢ Kale
- ➢ Olives
- ➢ Chickpeas

- Red Bell Pepper
- Jalapeno Pepper
- Onion
- Mushrooms
- Chipotle Peppers
- Cauliflower
- Green Beans
- Chives

Cooking Items

- Chia Seeds
- Cacao Nibs
- Old-fashioned oats
- Vanilla Extract
- Coconut Flakes
- Wheat Bread
- Maple Syrup
- Pine Nuts
- Walnuts
- Quinoa
- Vegetable Broth
- Garlic Cloves
- Tortilla Chips
- Lime Juice
- Extra-firm Tofu

- ➢ Red Curry Paste
- ➢ Soy Sauce
- ➢ Hoisin Sauce

Spices

- ➢ Ground Cinnamon
- ➢ Rosemary
- ➢ Garlic Powder
- ➢ Cumin
- ➢ Smoked Paprika

Plant-Based Dairy

- ➢ Almond Milk
- ➢ Plant-based Cheese

As you learn how to meal prep for yourself, you will learn how to use Ingredients in multiple recipes. It may seem slightly difficult at first, but remember that there is no shame in keeping your meal plans simple. One of my favorite dishes is a bowl with brown rice, corn, and black beans! It is ready in five minutes and delicious, despite only being three Ingredients!

Breakfast

For breakfast during the last week of your kickstart, I want you to focus on getting your vitamins and minerals in, first thing! That is why I placed superfood breakfast bowls and fruit smoothies for breakfast. Each one of these recipes will pack fruits and vegetables into your very first meal of the day. Plus, for a little treat at the end of your final week, plant-based French toast!

Lunch

As far as lunches go for your final week, your goal for lunch should be consuming leftovers. By learning how to incorporate leftovers into your meal plan, this will ensure that you can stick to a budget, and no food will go to waste! Leftovers can be excellent to provide variety through the week when you don't feel like putting together a salad. While I have mentioned the Kale Salad for this specific meal plan, feel free to use any of the salad recipes provided in this book!

Dinner

Last but not least, we have dinner time. As you can tell from the week 3 guide, there are multiple recipes that include tofu. Tofu is going to be a brilliant way to incorporate more protein into your macros. The best aspect of Tofu is how versatile it is. As you follow the plant-based diet, you will learn multiple ways to cook and enjoy tofu!

Dessert

During your final week of the kick-start, I invite you to enjoy dessert!

When starting any new diet, you will want to focus on changing your habits, not just your food choices. While it seems like a good idea to cut out sweets and desserts altogether, sometimes it isn't a realistic goal. Instead, you will want to provide yourself with a dessert that is healthy and something you can keep in moderation.

If you do want to include dessert during the final week of your plant-based kickstart, I recommend one of the following.

- Baked Cinnamon Apples
- Sweet Chia Pudding
- Plant-based Peanut Butter Cookies

- Coconut Dessert Balls

When the third week is over, you are now going to be on your own! While it may seem overwhelming at first, remember to take each day step by step. Throughout your day, you are going to have to make multiple food choices for yourself. Whether you have a plan or not, try to remember to pack your dish with plants, and you will be on your way in the right direction!

CHAPTER 13:

Sticking to the Plan

While we all know that there are some incredible benefits that come along with sticking to a meal plan, it is often easier said than done! If you are ready to create a meal plan and stick with it, here are my favorite tips and tricks to accomplishing your goals!

How to Stick to a Plan

What Are Your Goals?

Before you even think about following a meal plan, I cannot express how important it will be to establish your goals beforehand. Why do you even want to do this in the first place? You know there are benefits to meal planning, so why do you want to put forth the extra effort for yourself? Whether you want to do this to eat healthier, save money, stop wasting food, give yourself a proper reason to follow a plan in the first place.

Remember that creating a meal plan is going to take some extra effort and time. When you stray from these plans, you are wasting that hard work you put into a meal plan! To help avoid wasting your own time, give yourself achievable goals to keep you going!

Keep it Achievable

The keyword here is keeping your goals, and your meal plans achievable. When you are first starting out, it is perfectly understandable that you want to dive in headfirst. However, when we find things difficult, it is easy enough just to forget the whole thing. For that reason, I highly suggest you set some achievable goals for your diet. There is absolutely no reason you need to plan all twenty-something meals out for the entire week. Instead, consider only starting off by planning a couple of meals for the week. This may seem like a small step, but at least you aren't overwhelming yourself!

Schedule and Check-In

Unfortunately, life can be fairly unpredictable. While having a meal plan can be helpful, there is no point if you aren't going to stick with it. As you create your meal plan, it will be vital that you check in with your schedule. Yes, some things pop up, but there are other events that are planned for weeks in advance. If you have a work party, you won't have time to create a meal.

As you go through your week, you will want to check in with your meal plan constantly. This way, you will be able to make adjustments as needed. This will also help if you look a few days in advance and plan for any Ingredients you will need from the store. It is all about looking ahead and planning for success.

Be Flexible

When we are first starting out on any diet, it is all too easy to be hard on ourselves! Yes, you are going to create a plan, but that doesn't mean that you absolutely HAVE to stick it out. There are going to be those nights when you simply do not feel like having a specific meal or having last night's leftovers for lunch. For this reason, you will need to learn how to be flexible when it comes to your meals.

One way around this could be switching out your meals with another night! This way, you still most likely have the Ingredients that you need; you are just creating the meal a day or two earlier! This isn't a total fail and will keep you on the guidelines of your meal plan.

You will also need to learn how to be flexible for your schedule. There are going to be weeks that you get busy, and your schedule is going to change three, four times. For times like these, I highly suggest having multiple meals in the freezer. This way, you just have to take out the pre-made lunch/dinner, thaw it out, and you can still stick to your diet! Just remember that while it is important to have your goals in mind, try not to be so strict with yourself.

Plan for the Leftovers

One of the most common issues people run into when they first begin meal prepping is not planning for leftovers! Even if you are feeding a whole family, there will always be nights that you are going to have leftovers.

As you choose your recipes, keep leftovers in mind for your meal plan. If you plan ahead, this can lower the chances that you are going to waste any food during the week. This also serves as an excellent way to keep your fridge cleared from any excess foods.

One of my favorite tricks for leftovers is to have a pot-luck on Sunday! Normally, this is my day for meal prepping and planning for the following week. By having a pot-luck on Sunday, this helps me avoid cooking more on Sunday and also creates more room in my fridge for the food for the next week.

Enjoy Yourself

Another reason people fail in their diet is that they are absolutely miserable. When you are following a plant-based diet, you should never look at yourself as being in food jail! The more you learn about the diet, the more you will understand that you are fortunate to have all of these incredible foods to enjoy on your diet.

If you find meal prepping and planning difficult, try to find ways to make the process fun and exciting! Yes, it is going to take you several hours to research your first few meals plans, but with time, it will come much easier to you.

One of the best ways to make meal planning fun and exciting is to invite the whole family to help out. This way, you can create a meal plan to fit everyone's needs instead of just expecting them to eat whatever you provide.

If you are meal prepping for yourself, you may want to consider playing music or listening to your favorite podcast as you create your meal plan. Instead of looking at this time as a waste to just create a plan, remind yourself that you are being very productive and that it is going to help you in the long run!

Conclusion

Thank you for making it through to the end of *THE PLANT-BASED DIET MEAL PLAN*; let's hope it was informative and able to provide you with all of the tools you need to achieve your goals whatever they may be.

The next step is to utilize all of this incredible information that you have been handed! While starting anything new in life can seem next to impossible, it is much easier when you take the changes step by step. Remember that as you are first starting the plant-based diet, nobody is expecting you to make these changes overnight!

It is going to take a little bit of time and a lot of effort to begin changing your ways. Whether you start off by incorporating meatless Mondays or just eating one plant-based meal a week, this is going to help start you off in the right direction. Eventually, you will be eating plant-based without thinking twice about it!

If you enjoy the meal plan provided in this book, feel free to follow it as long as you need it! Eventually, I hope that you feel comfortable enough creating meal plans for yourself that are specifically tailored to your goals. Whether you are looking to improve your health, give your metabolism a boost, or lose weight, the plant-based diet can help you get there!

I highly suggest you give every recipe in this book at least one chance. As you expand your horizons, you will learn more about your own personal taste. Eventually, you will have a list of staple meals to keep your diet exciting and delicious. There are many recipes out there for your enjoyment; it is just a matter of finding them!

Finally, it is vital that you keep yourself motivated throughout your health journey. It is fairly easy in the beginning when you are fresh, but keep your WHY in mind as you keep following this lifestyle. It is time to say goodbye to yo-yo dieting and hello to a new and healthier lifestyle. Through the plant-based diet, you will be able to accomplish all of your health goals and live healthier than ever before. I hope you find the change you are looking for and enjoy your new diet.

If you found this book useful in any way, a review on Amazon is always appreciated!

BONUS:

Italian Recipes

As a bonus for my readers, I decided to include a bonus chapter based around my favorite Italian Recipes! While many feel this may be hard to accomplish due to the amount of cheese and oil used in Italian, you may be surprised to learn just how delicious plant-based Italian recipes can still be!

Pesto Gnocchi

Yield: [Two]

Prepping: [Ten Minutes]

Ingredients

- Toasted Pine Nuts [3 T.]
- Fresh Basil [1 C.]
- Gnocchi [1 Package]
- Arugula [3 C.]
- Asparagus [1 C.]
- Lemon Juice [1 T.]
- Salt [Dash]
- Garlic Clove [1]
- Pepper [Dash]

Directions

1. When first starting this recipe, you will want first to make your own pesto. While store-bought pesto can be convenient, it is often not plant-based friendly. Luckily, the recipe is very simple! You are going to start off by roasting your garlic clove over a moderate temperature. Once browned, you will toss it into your food processor along with the basil, pine nuts, lemon juice, and ¼ cup of water.

2. Once your pesto sauce is made, you will want to go ahead and make the gnocchi according to the instructions on the package. When the gnocchi is cooked to your liking, you will want to drain and toss generously in your pesto sauce.

3. Finally, dash a little bit of seasoning over the top, and your meal will be set for your enjoyment.

Eggplant Tomato Parm

Yield: [Four]

Prepping: [Thirty Minutes]

Ingredients

- Tomatoes [2, Sliced]
- Italian Breadcrumbs [1 C.]
- Eggplant [1, Sliced]
- Water [3 T.]
- Pepper [Dash]

Directions

1. While you may think that making Parm is going to take you forever, it is simpler than you will believe! To start this delicious recipe out, you will want to put your broiler on the highest setting.

2. As the oven warms up, you will want to go ahead and slice up your vegetables according to the direction. If you like your eggplant crispier, you will need to take several minutes to sprinkle salt over the eggplant to draw out excess moisture. Generally, this step will only take you an additional five minutes.

3. When your vegetables are set, lay them across a baking sheet and pop it into the stove for six minutes. After six minutes, remove the dish from the stove and flip all of the pieces over. At this point, you will season with some pepper and salt and broil for an additional ten minutes.

4. Next, you will want to take out two mixing bowls. One for the water and one for the breadcrumbs. When the vegetables are cooked to your liking, carefully dip each piece into the water and roll in the breadcrumbs. When this step is complete, place the pieces back onto the dish and place it in the stove for an additional five minutes.

5. Finally, remove from the stove, allow to cool slightly, and enjoy!

Basil Tomato Risotto

Yield: [Four]

Prepping: [One Hour]

Ingredients

- Vegetable Broth [3 C.]
- Garlic Cloves [2, Minced]
- Dry White Wine [.25 C.]
- Arborio Rice [1 C.]
- Basil [1 T., Chopped]
- Tomatoes [1 C., Chopped]
- Salt [Dash]
- Onion [.50 C.]
- Sundried Tomatoes [.50 C.]
- Tomato Paste [1 T.]

Directions

1. Risotto is a delicious, classic Italian recipe. Now, you will know how to make your own from home! To begin this recipe, you will want to get out your cooking pan and place it over a moderate temperature. When you have done this, go ahead and sauté the garlic cloves and onions for several minutes. When these are cooked to your liking, you will also add in the tomatoes and rice.

2. When these Ingredients are set, you will then pour in the white wine and allow for this liquid to become completely absorbed. Once it has been, add in one cup of your vegetable stock along with the sun-dried tomatoes, tomato paste, and the basil. Eventually, the rice will absorb the vegetable stock as well.

3. Once the step from above is complete, add another half cup of your stock and continuously stir everything and keep adding in the stock until you have used all three cups. After this point, leave your rice over a moderate temperature for an additional thirty minutes.

4. If you feel your risotto is too dry, add as much vegetable stock as you feel necessary. When it has reached your desired texture, remove the pan from the heat, and enjoy your recipe immediately.

Vegetable Cauliflower Risotto

Yield: [Four]

Prepping: [Thirty Minutes]

Ingredients

- Cauliflower [1 Head]
- Garlic Cloves [3]
- Mushrooms [1 C., Sliced]
- Spinach [4 C.]
- Salt [Dash]
- Fresh Thyme [4 Sprigs]
- Onion [.25 C.]
- Vegetable Stock [.50 C.]
- Pepper [Dash]

Directions

1. If you are looking for a recipe that is going to keep your carb-count low, you will want to try this risotto! To begin, you will want to cut your cauliflower into smaller pieces and then place it into a food processor to create your "rice."

2. Next, you will want to get out your cooking pan and put it over a moderate temperature. Once warm, begin cooking the onion and mushrooms until they are tender. As they cook, feel free to season with the pepper, salt, garlic, and thyme.

3. Finally, you are going to add in the cauliflower rice along with the vegetable stock. Go ahead and cook these together for five minutes or until the vegetable stock has been completely absorbed.

4. At this point, you can portion out your risotto and garnish with some fresh thyme for a kick of extra flavor! This recipe works perfect by itself or make up quickly for a healthy side dish.

Creamy Tomato Pasta

Yield: [Four]

Prepping: [Forty Minutes]

Ingredients

- Coconut Milk [1 Can]
- Onion [1, Diced]
- Tomato [1, Diced]
- Cayenne Powder [.25 t.]
- Paprika Powder [.25 t.]
- Parsley [.25 C., Chopped]
- Basil [.25 C., Chopped]
- Garlic Cloves [2, Diced]
- Tomato [.50 C.]
- Pasta [3 C.]

Directions

1. Creamy, filling, and delicious! To begin this recipe, get out your baking pan and put it over a moderate temperature. When it is warm, splash in some water and begin sautéing your garlic and onion for three or four minutes. After this time has passed, add in the spices along with the tomatoes and cook for an additional ten minutes.

2. Finally, you are going to add in the coconut milk and simmer the Ingredients over a lowered temperature for thirty minutes. After the thirty minutes have passed, carefully pour everything into a food processor and blend for thirty seconds, or until smooth.

3. Now that your sauce has been made, you will want to go ahead and make your pasta of choice according to the instructions on the package. When this is all set, drain out the water and pour in your tomato sauce. For best results, simmer these Ingredients together for five minutes before portioning out your meal and serving!

Mushroom and Garlic Pasta

Yield: [Two]

Prepping: [Thirty Minutes]

Ingredients

- Almond Milk [2 C.]
- Corn Flour [2 T.]
- Onion [.50 C., Diced]
- Mushrooms [.50 C., Sliced]
- Nutritional Yeast [1.50 T.]
- Water [3 T.]
- Pasta [4 C.]
- Garlic Cloves [2, Diced]
- Salt [Dash]

Directions

1. To make this delicious recipe in a short amount of time, you will have to start out by multi-tasking. First, go ahead and cook the pasta the way you normally would. After this is set, drain the water and place the cooked pasta to the side.

2. As the pasta cooks, get out your frying pan and put it over a moderate temperature. Once warm, toss in your onion pieces and sauté for five minutes. When the onions are cooked to your liking, sprinkle in the cornflour and the almond milk. You will notice a sauce begin to thicken, and then you can dash in some salt and nutritional yeast.

3. When the step from above is complete, you will add all of the Ingredients into a blender or food processor along with the garlic. Go ahead and process these items until smooth and then set it to the side.

4. Next, it is time to cook the mushrooms. You will want to use the pan you used from earlier and sauté these for about five minutes. When the mushrooms are soft, place your sauce back into the pan and turn your temperature down to low.

5. As the sauce begins to simmer, this is when you will want to add in the pasta and coat it generously with your sauce. At this point, you will also want to season the dish according to your own taste.

6. Once the pasta is heated thoroughly, portion out into your serving dishes, top with some fresh parsley, and enjoy your quick and easy Italian meal!

Easy Creamy Avocado Pasta

Yield: [Four]

Prepping: [Twenty Minutes]

Ingredients

- Penne Pasta [3 C.]
- Lemon Juice [1 T.]
- Avocado [1, Sliced]
- Water [1 t.]
- Spinach [1 C.]
- Pepper [Dash]
- Chili Flakes [.10 t.]
- Salt [Dash]

Directions

1. While many people don't think of using avocado when they are cooking Italian, it is the perfect way to make any sauce nice and creamy. To recreate this recipe, your first step is going to be making your penne pasta according to the instructions provided on the package. When this is complete, set the pasta to the side.

2. Next, it is time to make your avocado sauce. You can complete this task by placing the avocado along with some water, spinach, garlic, lemon juice, and seasoning into your food processor. After processing for thirty seconds, you will have your creamy avocado sauce almost in an instant!

3. When you are set to make your meal, get out a sauce pot and begin heating the sauce that you just made. Generally, this should only take you about five minutes. Once warm, you will carefully stir in your cooked penne and coat each piece as generously as possible.

4. Once you are set, portion out your pasta and enjoy!

Plant-Based Lasagna

Yield: [Ten]

Prepping: [Forty Minutes]

Ingredients

- Lasagna Noodles [12 Pieces]
- Spinach [3 C.]
- Zucchini [1, Chopped]
- Marinara Sauce [6 C.]
- Peas [1 C.]
- Hummus [1 C.]
- Extra-firm Tofu [1 Package]
- Fresh Basil [.25 C.]
- Nutritional Yeast [.50 C.]
- Salt [Dash]
- Mushrooms [1 C., Sliced]
- Pepper [Dash]
- Garlic Powder [1 t.]

Directions

1. While lasagna can be a more difficult recipe to make, it is worth putting forth the time and the effort for such a delicious meal! To begin this recipe, you will want to prep your stove to 350 and also begin boiling a pot of water so that you can cook your lasagna noodles.

2.   Next, it is time to cook your vegetables. You can complete this step by taking out your cooking pan and placing it over a moderate temperature. When the pan is warm, add in your mushrooms and zucchini. When these items are in place, season to your liking and sauté for five minutes.

3.   Once the zucchini and mushrooms are cooked, you will next toss in the peas and spinach. After you have cooked these Ingredients for an additional five minutes, take the pan from the heat and set it to the side.

4.   Next, it is time to make the tofu ricotta for the lasagna. Before you begin cooking this, you will want to take several minutes to drain to tofu properly. When this has been completed, crumble the tofu with your hands and place into a bowl with the garlic powder, salt, basil, hummus, and the nutritional yeast. As you begin to stir these Ingredients together, you will notice it looks a lot like ricotta!

5.   Now, you are finally ready to assemble your dish. You will want to start out by taking out a baking dish and layering about a cup and a half of the marinara sauce on the bottom. When this is in place, layer some noodles across the sauce along with half a cup of the ricotta mixture and another half of a cup of your cooked vegetables. When these are placed, you will add more sauce and continue the layering process until you run out.

6.   When you are set with the layering, feel free to sprinkle some more nutritional yeast over the top. Once you are ready to cook your meal, you will want to cover the baking dish with some tin foil before popping into the stove for thirty minutes.

7.   After thirty minutes, remove the dish from the stove and permit it to chill for ten minutes or so before slicing and serving.

Made in the USA
Monee, IL
29 February 2020